Page 37
missing

Page 37
missing

# NASCAR LEGENDS

DON HUNTER AND BEN WHITE

Crestline

## CRESTLINE

An imprint of MBI Publishing Company

The edition published in 2004 by Crestline, an imprint of MBI Publishing Company, Galtier Plaza, Suite 200, 380 Jackson Street, St. Paul, MN 55101-3885 USA

First published in 1997 by MBI Publishing Company as *American Stock Car Racers*

Crestline books are also available at discounts in bulk quantity for industrial or sales-promotional use. For details, please contact: Special Sales Manager at MBI Publishing Company, Galtier Plaza, Suite 200, 380 Jackson Street, St. Paul, MN 55101-3885 USA.

For a free catalog, call 1-800-826-6600, or visit our website at www.motorbooks.com.

ISBN 0-7603-1804-2

All photos by Don Hunter unless otherwise noted

Printed in China

# CONTENTS

| | |
|---|---|
| Acknowledgments | 6 |
| Introduction | 7 |
| Bobby Allison | 9 |
| Davey Allison | 15 |
| Donnie Allison | 17 |
| Elzie Wylie "Buddy" Baker | 23 |
| Neil Bonnett | 27 |
| Henry Neil "Soapy" Castles | 29 |
| Dale Earnhardt | 33 |
| Bill Elliott | 39 |
| Tim Flock | 43 |
| Bill France, Sr. | 45 |
| Jeff Gordon | 47 |
| John Holman and Ralph Moody | 49 |
| Ernie Irvan | 55 |
| Robert Vance Isaac | 57 |
| Dale Jarrett | 61 |
| Ned Jarrett | 63 |
| Junior Johnson | 65 |
| Alan Kulwicki | 71 |
| Terry Labonte | 73 |
| Fred Lorenzen | 77 |
| Tiny Lund | 81 |
| Dave Marcis | 85 |
| Sterling Marlin | 87 |
| Mark Martin | 89 |
| Everette Douglas "Cotton" Owens | 91 |
| Benny Parsons | 93 |
| David Pearson | 97 |
| Kyle Petty | 101 |
| Richard Petty | 103 |
| Tim Richmond | 109 |
| Glenn "Fireball" Roberts | 111 |
| Ricky Rudd | 115 |
| Ken Schrader | 117 |
| Wendell Scott | 119 |
| Curtis Turner | 123 |
| Rusty Wallace | 127 |
| Darrell Waltrip | 129 |
| Joe Weatherly | 133 |
| Glen and Leonard Wood | 135 |
| Cale Yarborough | 139 |
| Lee Roy Yarbrough | 145 |
| Henry "Smokey" Yunick | 147 |
| More Great Moments | 150 |
| Index | 160 |

# ACKNOWLEDGMENTS

During the rather short but creatively prosperous period in which this book was written, several people offered much needed support, advice, and encouragement to finish the project.

I would especially like to thank my wife, Eva, and our son, Aaron, for allowing me time away from my loving duties as husband and father. Both were extremely patient with me when writing time took precedence over family time. You are both the loves of my life. Your tremendous support and understanding means so very much to me.

Many thanks to Whitney Shaw, Group Publisher for Street and Smith's Sports Group for allowing the use of *NASCAR Winston Cup Illustrated* and *American Racing Classics* as reference material for this book, as well as much gratitude to Greg Fielden for his series, *40 Years of Stock Car Racing*.

I would like to thank Steve Waid for his invaluable advice on subject matter as well his help making the words flow with ease. You've been a great friend to me over the years and it's been an honor to have you at my side for our second book together.

Also, I extend appreciation to Betty Carlan, Deb Williams, Gene Granger, and Gary McCredie for helping to provide information on those featured in this book.

Then there are those competitors who offered their comments; Bobby Allison, Donnie Allison, Buddy Baker, Richard Childress, Lee Holman, Ned Jarrett, Fred Lorenzen, Dave Marcis, Sterling Marlin, Larry McReynolds, Benny Parsons, David Pearson, Richard Petty, Doris Roberts, Rusty Wallace, Darrell Waltrip, Len Wood, and Cale Yarborough.

Many thanks to Don Hunter for the striking photography he has provided for this book. These pages come to life through his brilliant creativity and his obvious passion for the sport. Through this project, a longtime professional association has become even stronger.

I'm very grateful to Lee Klancher, the editor I worked with at Motorbooks International, for his steadfast patience and advice throughout the creation of this project. Best of all, a friendship has emerged between us that I'm sure will last for many years to come. Thanks also to Desk Editor Tracy Snyder, whose attention to detail ensured that every "i" was dotted and "t" was crossed.

Without your support, this book could not have come together.

Ben White
June 1997


I would like to thank Humpy Wheeler, president of Charlotte Motor Speedway; NASCAR for all the doors they opened for me; Chrysler Corporation; Ford Motor Company; General Motors Corporation; Brock Yates of Car and Driver; David E. Davis; Dick Berggren of Stock Car Racing; the late Jack Sheedy, a fellow Chrysler photographer and good friend—we found a lot of good locations and "magic light" over the years; all the drivers I worked with at events and especially Richard Petty, who heads the list.

Thanks to my wife, Jean, who traveled with me for the last half of my career and was my secretary, accountant, assistant, and model coordinator. I couldn't have done it without all these people, especially Jean.

Don Hunter
June 1997

# INTRODUCTION

Having to capsulize any notable athlete's career in just over 1,000 words is extremely difficult and could even be considered an art form in itself.

So it is with the careers of the subjects chosen for this book. They are careers which are colorful and insightful, full of accomplishments and stories that helped form stock car racing's history and lore. What is written in these pages are mere glimpses of a few of those athletes who laid the groundwork for NASCAR's overwhelming success today. There are many, many others just as deserving as those featured here. Perhaps their stories will be told one day.

The subjects selected for this chronicle came to these pages after a great deal of conversation and many hours of deliberation. The result, we trust, is a representation of several eras of NASCAR's existence.

The overall theme for *American Stock Car Racers* was to present each individual in such a way that readers could get to know them on a more personal basis through photos and the written word. They, like us, were average folks, many of whom came right out of the cotton field or mill to feed a hunger for a better life. Existences were tough, as the big money and big sponsorships were not to come to stock car racing until many years later.

Often, those who raced stock cars did so after gaining experience hauling moonshine through the mountains of the Southeast. It was a way to supplement family income, but the price paid if caught by Federal agents was harsh. As an option, one could drive a stock car fast and perhaps win that necessary money for the family. As it evolved, some of the more enterprising pioneer stock car drivers funded their racing efforts by hauling and selling moonshine on the side.

These are the individuals who make up the foundation upon which NASCAR built and, in fact, stands today. These early stock car drivers risked their lives for little monetary gain and even less public recognition. Still, the ability to best a rival on an in turn or down a straightaway—whether it be in some lonely country cow pasture or on the high banks of Daytona International Speedway—was their motivation. Without the sacrifices of the subjects featured in these pages, NASCAR racing simply wouldn't exist.

For more than one driver, stock car racing provided a way to find identity: a sense of who he was and what he could be. Without the sport, the choices were few. And it evolved that many drivers found a certain degree of celebrity status simply by doing what they enjoyed most.

The highest of triumphs and lowest of disappointments can be seen in their eyes and actions captured by the photographs within these pages. Seconds in time have been recorded on film.

A reader can travel back in time and visit those who have departed, some due to racing accidents. Through these pages is offered a special opportunity for everyone to reminisce on the glory days, and the glorious careers, that have passed.

It is our hope this book will help keep a special innocence that stock car racing once enjoyed alive forever.

# BOBBY ALLISON 1937-

At 14 years of age, Robert Arthur "Bobby" Allison found himself underneath the hood of an old T-model Ford belonging to the headmaster of his Catholic school. His fascination with the mechanical workings of automobiles had gained him a side job or two tuning up engines for friends and family.

When the headmaster saw the feet of the young Allison sticking out underneath his car, he asked, "Mr. Allison? Have you found the problem?"

In a muffled voice, Allison replied, "No."

Again, the headmaster asked, "I say, Mr. Allison, have you found the problem?"

Irritated by the pestering, the young mechanic said, "Hell, no!" Then his eyes met the headmaster's dark shoes and trousers and followed the pant crease up to his collar and the scowl above it.

Allison began to apologize profusely, vowing never to speak with a profane tongue again. It was the first time he spoke his mind concerning the automobile before him, but it would not be the last.

Allison hadn't intended to drive stock cars for a living; as a teenager, work with his father's hydraulic car-lift business kept him busy on weekends. One weekend, however, an uncle treated Allison to a stock car race at the local fairgrounds. After an evening of watching old modifieds stir up dirt, Allison was hooked. From then on, every spare moment was spent studying the cars and the drivers. The urge to drive was nearly uncontrollable.

For Allison to compete as a race car driver, he had to work to raise the money for his first car, which he drove to school during the week and to the race track on Saturday. This arrangement worked just fine until he was required to produce a written parental permission slip to compete.

After night after night of begging his mother for permission, she finally relented. While she thought her blessings were for one race, Allison considered it permission for, as he puts it, "at least 100 years."

The odds on a second permission slip were slim, so Allison borrowed the license of a friend, Bob Sunoman, to help launch his career. He used an assumed name, and each time he won, the local newspapers credited the win to "Bob Sunderman."

The sham ended when his father read the newspaper one Sunday afternoon and saw his son's photo and fictitious name accompanying

a story announcing another victory. Allison's dad confronted Bobby, saying, "If you're going to race, use your own name," and gave his approval. Bobby's mother was not so easy to win over, but she finally gave in.

The wins continued, and Allison graduated to the modified ranks where he was crowned national champion twice. Around his Florida home, Allison won almost everything there was to offer.

A break from his racing sent him to work with another uncle at the Mercury Outboard test facility owned by NASCAR team owner Carl Kiekhaefer. During an engine test, Allison's boat turned over in the icy water, and he nearly drowned. A nurse who lived on the lake came to his rescue and gave him immediate first aid for his frozen body.

Once at the hospital, the doctor treating Allison recognized the victim, as he announced, "I know you're the patient because you're wearing my clothes."

He returned home soon after and continued his racing. Through conversations with other drivers, he was informed that tracks in Alabama paid more money across the board, so Allison and his brother Donnie moved there, leaving their roots behind.

By 1961, Ralph Stark, Allison's brother-in-law, offered Allison a ride for the Daytona 500. There he started 36th and finished 31st in the 58-car field. It was his first NASCAR start, with 716 more to come.

In 1965, Allison fielded his own cars, battling the highly financed Winston Cup teams on a shoestring budget. The following year, he scored three victories and finished 10th in NASCAR's point standings. Many were impressed, including Ford Motor Company and its stock car racing arm, headed by John Holman and Ralph Moody. Allison was given his first top ride, but he and Holman had nothing in common. Thus began the first of Allison's several rocky relationships with team owners. His opinions seemed to turn owners against him, but his ability on the race track made up for many of his shortcomings.

In cars owned by Allison, Mario Rossi, Richard Howard, Roger Penske, Bud Moore, Harry Ranier, Bill and Jim Gardner, and Bill and Mickey Stavola, Allison won 86 races in eight car makes over a 27-year span, including three Daytona 500 wins, four Southern 500 wins at Darlington, South Carolina, and the 1983 Winston Cup championship.

Then, seemingly overnight, his world turned upside down.

On June 19, 1988, Allison was forced into retirement when a cut tire caused his car to spin into the outside retaining wall during the opening laps of a race at Pocono International Raceway in Pennsylvania. While he sat stopped on the track, his car was struck in the driver's side door. Weeks after the crash, he remained in critical condition, followed by months of intensive physical therapy. He is still suffering physical problems and memory loss.

His youngest son and aspiring driver, Clifford Allison, died on August 13, 1992, in a crash during a practice session at Michigan International Raceway. Just 11 months later, his oldest son, Davey, a racing star in his own right, died as a result of injuries suffered in a helicopter crash at Talladega Superspeedway in Alabama.

In 1990, Allison fielded his own race team, this time from a shop in Charlotte, North Carolina, for the third time in his career. Over time, he employed several drivers. But after 207 starts with only three second-place finishes on the record, the team stopped operating at the end of the 1996 season.

"My career is a situation that started with a guy who really wanted to do something so bad that he would have paid people to let him run on their race track," Allison says. "If they had known that, Bobby Allison would have never gotten any prize money. I had a lot of people to help me early on, and we put a lot of effort into it. We had our share of success.

"I think of the good times. I think of the bad times. I think about the people I raced for and won for, only to get fired. I think of the other people I worked so hard for and couldn't really get that success we wanted. Still, I ended up with a lot of wins and a lot of good times and was able to share that with a lot of people.

"The championship I won in 1983 has to be the greatest thing going," Allison said. "And if I could ever remember the 1988 Daytona 500 where a 50-year-old guy wins the race over his son, that's got to be a super deal.

"I've been all the way to the top of the mountain and also all the way to the bottom of the valley, but all those things were very small compared to losing my two sons. Davey died in a helicopter and Clifford in a race car, but I still lost them. The greatest compliment a parent can have is to know their child is loved around the world."

After an intense afternoon in the heat of battle, Bobby Allison is given information concerning another engine gone bad.

Allison takes a break in his Bondy Long Ford during the 1968 season. Later that year, he returned to fielding his own cars.

Allison with his family during the early years of his career. From left to right, he is joined by his former wife, Judy, and children, Clifford, Bonnie, Carrie, and Davey.

Allison muscles his way through turn four at Charlotte Motor Speedway while chasing Lee Roy Yarbrough in the 1970 National 500. In the end, his Mario Rossi-owned Dodge finished second after a caution in the final laps.

During one of his most successful seasons, Allison makes a pit stop at Rockingham, North Carolina, in 1972 while driving a Chevrolet for team owner Richard Howard and car builder and crew chief Junior Johnson. It was Allison's 10th win of the season.

Allison found himself under the hood of his Matadors many times during the 1977 season. It was one of the most trying years of his career.

Allison's last Winston Cup victory came in the 1988 Daytona 500 over his son, Davey, at the checkered flag.

Allison tugs his helmet strap with gloved hands during a cold test session and Media Tour appearance at Charlotte Motor Speedway. Ironically, the photo was taken the day of the explosion of the space shuttle Challenger in January 1986.

Allison celebrates with his son, Davey, who just won his first superspeedway victory in ARCA competition at Talladega Superspeedway in 1983.

# DAVEY ALLISON 1961-1993

Through the back glass of a battle-scarred pickup truck, two-year-old David Carl "Davey" Allison would gaze at his father's race car being towed on the trailer behind. Too young to speak, he would simply point to the modified racer and utter sounds of a running engine. The jabbering kept his father, Bobby Allison, awake during the long rides between Miami and wherever the elder Allison was racing.

When young Davey tired of the game, the two-year-old would fall quietly into his mother's arms and instantly drift off to sleep.

Davey Allison knew of nothing but race cars during his 32 years of life. While in class during his elementary school years, he was constantly reprimanded for drawing pictures of race cars during times when he should have been paying attention to the lesson.

When the time came to build his own race cars, the shop and the equipment in it were at Davey's disposal with his father's blessing—but not much else. If the young man was going to make it, it had to be on his own, without trading off the Allison name. There was no other way to learn.

Davey's high school grades suffered at times, once to the point where his parents banned him from racing until the marks improved. Once they did, the shop doors were open to him again.

He sorted nuts and bolts and swept floors for his father's Winston Cup effort in the afternoons and on weekends, all the while wishing his name was the one painted on the rooflines of the cars around him. Being on the company payroll gave him minimal financing for his own car.

Once Davey started driving, the wins eventually came on short tracks across the Southeast. The desire to go Winston Cup racing was stronger than ever; but timing was everything, his father warned.

So there came more short track races and more short track wins. Finally, on July 28, 1985, Allison drove a Hoss Ellington–owned Chevrolet to a 10th-place finish at Talladega Superspeedway for his Winston Cup debut. As he rolled to a stop in the garage area, the press crowded around the young man many believed would be the sport's next superstar.

Allison made limited appearances throughout the 1986 season, and a substitution for an injured Neil Bonnett in the Junior Johnson-owned Chevrolet produced an impressive seventh-place finish. The respectable result was enough to silence any remaining critics who felt he couldn't handle a top ride.

Davey Allison talking strategy with his Harry Ranier racing crew.

On the low side of turn four at North Wilkesboro Speedway, Allison drifts through the corner with ease in his Robert Yates Ford.

Yates and the young Allison formed a complementary team. Both were soft-spoken, slightly to deeply introverted, intensely competitive, and had appetites for winning.

By September of that year, Allison came to Darlington dressed in a flannel shirt and jeans and without a ride, but the news he carried within him made him beam. He had signed a contract to run the full 1987 schedule with team owner Harry Ranier as the replacement driver for the departing Cale Yarborough.

His dark eyes danced wildly when he spoke of his newfound fortune, as he knew it would be only a matter of time before the success his father had enjoyed would finally come to him. The union produced two victories and Rookie of the Year honors. No other driver since has won a race in his or her rookie season.

With the departure of Ranier in 1988 came Robert Yates, the multi-talented engine builder who moved from crew chief to team owner and businessman. Yates and the young Allison formed a complementary team. Both were soft-spoken, slightly to deeply introverted, intensely competitive, and had appetites for winning. They were like two lost sheep who had found their home. The pair produced 17 victories, including the 1992 Daytona 500, 14 pole positions, and several impressive runs at the Winston Cup championship.

Even though the crown never came to them, Yates and Allison had much to be proud of. Allison confided to his closest friends his desire to finish his career with Yates. Ironically, he did just that.

Allison died on July 13, 1993, from injuries suffered in a helicopter that crashed while attempting to land at Talladega Superspeedway one day earlier. His passenger, longtime racer and crew chief Red Farmer, suffered broken bones and bruises, but was not seriously injured.

"Davey was a great competitor and a great friend," says Larry McReynolds, Allison's former crew chief. "There isn't a day that goes by that I don't think about him. We had some awesome successes together, but more importantly, he was a great human being to get to know. He was quite an individual."

# DONNIE ALLISON 1939-

A Florida State Diving Champion in 1954, Donnie Allison followed his older brother, Bobby, into NASCAR Winston Cup racing. He was determined to make a name for himself, partly because his older brother said he'd never be a race driver. Donnie Allison's name became a household word in both stock cars and Indy cars. He was known not only for his driving, but also for his outspoken manner. When conflicts arose, Allison could, at times, voiced heated opinions.

Ever since the days of growing up on 19th Street on the north side of Miami, Florida, Allison had to stand his ground. He was the sixth of 13 children in the Allison household, so exposure to tough competition was nothing new. He learned from an early age to treat those around him fairly and never waiver from his beliefs. That schooling set his personality in motion on occasion when a NASCAR ruling was being placed against him.

As a young man, he learned to spend his money wisely. When he and Bobby were pulling their modified coupes up and down the East Coast, they would buy bushels of peaches and eat them for breakfast, lunch, and dinner to stretch the money in their pockets. If they had to choose between food and parts, the race car came first. He sold a shotgun his father gave him for $35 to finance his move to Alabama. At that time, $35 was just as good as $10,000.

Allison eventually graduated to the NASCAR Winston Cup (then Grand National) circuit in 1966 with two starts that year. On October 16, 1966, he qualified a 1965 Chevrolet owned by Robert Harper in 39th position at Charlotte Motor Speedway and finished 27th. Two weeks later, he scored his first top-10 finish with a 9th-place run at North Carolina Motor Speedway.

Allison's first victory came on June 16, 1968, at Rockingham, North Carolina, while behind the wheel of a Banjo Matthews-owned Ford. At the end, Allison had bested his brother Bobby by a two-lap margin. A third brother, Eddie, served as crew chief for Bobby as well as third-place driver James Hylton.

The best year of his career was 1970. In Matthew's Fords, Allison won at Bristol, Tennessee, in April; Charlotte, North Carolina, in May; and Daytona in July. Of those wins, the Charlotte triumph was his biggest. Allison called upon Lee Roy Yarbrough for relief, and his replacement took the lead on lap 363 of the 400-lap event and never looked back.

Allison was victorious only once in 1971. At Talladega. Alabama, in the Winston 500, he

again bested his older brother to the checkered flag while driving a Mercury for team owner Glen Wood and chief mechanic Leonard Wood. From there, Allison suffered a long five-year drought before finding victory lane for Hoss Ellington on October 10, 1976, at Charlotte.

The win at Charlotte carried some serious controversy.

After a postrace inspection of his car's engine, Allison, Ellington, and NASCAR's technical director, Bill Gazaway, got into a heated argument concerning the engine's displacement, which appeared to the officials to be just a fraction over the 358-cubic-inch limit man-

---

> When [Donnie] and Bobby were pulling their modified coupes up and down the East Coast, they would buy bushels of peaches and eat them for breakfast, lunch, and dinner to stretch the money in their pockets.

---

dated by NASCAR. The engine cooled for several hours and was inspected again. The results of the second test found it was within NASCAR specifications. Still, Allison was boiling, as he felt NASCAR's way of checking the engine was primitive and inconclusive.

A. J. Foyt, Ellington's full-time driver, quit the team after the Charlotte event, citing his unhappiness over a two-car effort, especially since he didn't feel his car was totally prepared to race. Foyt quit the ride, giving the driving duties to Allison.

Allison won at Talladega, Alabama, on August 7, 1977, with relief help from Darrell Waltrip. Another win came on October 23 of that year at Rockingham, North Carolina.

Allison's last career victory came on November 5, 1978, at Atlanta, Georgia, after a scoring error marred the event. Initially, the win was awarded to Richard Petty, but score cards were checked and rechecked. At 7:40 P.M. the decision was placed in Allison's favor. The Florida native had passed Petty and third place Dave Marcis, but both his scorers were wrong on their counts. Allison discovered he was the winner after he returned home to Alabama.

On May 24, 1981, Allison suffered the worst accident of his career. During the 152nd lap of the World 600 at Charlotte, his car slid sideways and slammed into the outside retaining wall, right into the path of Dick Brooks. The two cars hit hard and, in doing so, left Allison with several broken ribs, a bruised right lung, a broken left knee, and a broken right shoulder blade. Brooks suffered a double fracture of his right shoulder.

The recovery period was lengthy. Allison returned to drive in a few races but was never in contention for the win. His last start came on August 21, 1988, at Michigan International Speedway. He started 41st and finished 35th.

"When I started out in Winston Cup, I was fortunate to win Rookie of the Year. It was a lot different than it is now. Evidently, I impressed some people and got a ride pretty quickly.

"Really, if I had it to do all over again, I might change the way I did things. I was happy with Donnie Allison. Maybe I should have had higher goals and that was to win races. I never really had the goal to win the championship."

"I ran modified specials and won track championships at all of them except one and I really didn't try to win them. I didn't go for that on purpose. All in all, with the exception of my injury (1981), I had up and down times. I accomplished an awful lot. I ran 241 Winston Cup races and had a pretty good career, especially with teams that didn't run every race."

Donnie Allison poses by his ride in 1970. Allison drove a 1969 Banjo Mathews Ford that year and won 3 races despite only 19 starts.

Allison takes his car around Charlotte, the site of his biggest 1970 victory which took place in the World 600 on May 24.

left: Allison (27) outdistances the aerodynamically superior Dodge Daytona of Buddy Baker (6) with his Banjo Matthews Ford at Charlotte Motor Speedway in 1970.

Allison enjoys a Sportsman victory at Daytona in the early 1970s.

Donny Allison (1) leads Richard Petty (43) in the closing laps of the National 500 at Charlotte Motor Speedway on October 11, 1976. Allison started the 334-lap event in the 15th position and was considered a dark horse for victory. He silenced the critics by pulling into victory lane only moments later, shown below. After the race, controversy erupted when his Hoss Ellington-owned Chevrolet was determined to have carried an oversized engine by five-eighths of a cubic inch. At the time, however, there was no engine measuring device that could determine such a measurement. The charge was later proven false and the win stood.

left: Allison cools off following his victory in the 1970 World 600 after receiving help from relief driver Lee Roy Yarbrough.

In 1976, Allison won the controversy-filled National 500 held at Charlotte Motor Speedway in a Hoss Ellington car that showed up without a major sponsor or high expectations of a win. The victory prompted a post-race inspection of the Ellington car (it passed on the second try) and saw Allison replace A.J. Foyt as the team driver.

# ELZIE WYLIE "BUDDY" BAKER 1941-

**W**ins didn't come often during Elzie Wylie "Buddy" Baker's illustrious career, but when they did come, they were big— very big!

Driving stock cars just as his dad did before him, it was pretty hard to miss Baker during any given race weekend. At 6 feet, 5 inches tall and weighing more than 200 pounds, he towered above most folks, both in physical stature and personality. He was well-liked by the racing fraternity, and the racing media dubbed him "The Gentle Giant."

Quick to offer humorous analogies, Baker's comical nature could have earned him a place on stage. When it came to racing, however, he took every lap seriously.

Born in Charlotte, North Carolina, the year World War II began, Baker knew from an early age his life's calling would involve racing stock cars. Growing up watching his father, Buck Baker, terrorize the tracks since the inception of the Winston Cup (then Grand National) circuit, Buddy Baker's desire to drive came naturally.

He finally got his chance at Columbia (South Carolina) Speedway on April 4, 1959. In that 200-lap event, young Buddy started 18th and finished 14th after suffering a broken shock absorber. Still, he finished five positions higher than his father, Buck, who was already a two-time NASCAR champion.

Several years of driving for his father provided much needed experience. More than 100 races passed before he landed his first top-quality ride, driving for Ray Fox, Sr. in 1966. It was the beginning of a special relationship that set the foundation for his career.

Baker's first victory came at Charlotte Motor Speedway on October 15, 1967. It was an underdog victory, as many of the front runners such as Gordon Johncock, Paul Goldsmith, Mario Andretti, Jim Paschal, and David Pearson all retired to the garage area. Baker had come into his own in front of the hometown crowd in one of NASCAR's most prestigious events.

In 1968, Baker found victory at Charlotte again in the grueling World 600 after rain shortened the race to 382.5 miles. Another major triumph came two years later in the 1970

Baker's 1969 Cotton Owens Dodge Daytona (6) battles closely with Pete Hamilton (40) in a 1970 Petty Enterprises Plymouth Superbird.

> He was well-liked by the racing fraternity, and the racing media dubbed him "The Gentle Giant."

Southern 500 at Darlington, South Carolina. Further wins at Darlington and Charlotte came for Baker while with Petty Enterprises in 1971 and 1972. Driving for Nord Krauskopf, Baker won at Nashville and Charlotte in 1973. With back-to-back World 600 victories, Baker's reputation as producer in high-exposure races was at an all-time high.

Team owners Bud Moore, M. C. Anderson, Harry Ranier, and the Wood Brothers hired the veteran for 11 more victories, his last coming at Daytona in July 1983. Of his 19 career wins, the 1980 Daytona 500 ranks as his biggest. It still ranks as the fastest Daytona 500 in history, averaging 177.602 miles per hour.

Baker once said, "You might say I won the Daytona 450 about 12 times," when commenting on so many 500s that slipped from his grasp. "I was in position to win that race so many times, but something would always happen. I wasn't sure I would ever get to victory lane there, but everything came together in 1980."

Baker retired from driving on April 3, 1993, and turned his attention to a second career in television broadcasting.

"I was lucky because I've enjoyed both sides of the windshield," Baker says. "I've driven race cars and then been able to tell about them through my broadcasting career.

"I've traveled the mountains and the valleys. I had four big wins at Charlotte and four big wins at Talladega and won the Daytona 500. Along the way, I was able to race against three generations of drivers.

"As the old saying goes, I've enjoyed the thrill of victory and the agony of defeat. I pinch myself every day because I've lived a charmed life."

Buddy Baker became a prominent figure in NASCAR in 1967 with his first career victory at Charlotte while driving a Dodge for team owner Ray Fox.

Baker receives fast pit work while driving a Dodge for Cotton Owens in 1970.

Baker exits his Petty Enterprises Dodge after racing 600 miles to victory at Charlotte on May 28, 1972.

As if studying the track surface and the line he must travel, Baker gathers his thoughts before race time.

Baker takes a moment with the late crew chief Harry Hyde during Speedweeks in February 1973 at Daytona. The two enjoyed much superspeedway success together.

# NEIL BONNETT 1947-1994

In April 1979, Neil Bonnett found himself in some pretty tight quarters. The racer in him dictated that he put stock cars aside briefly and try to make the starting field for the Indianapolis 500. Stuffed tighter than a size 12 foot in a size 10 shoe into an Indy car owned by Warner Hodgdon, Bonnett sat and waited for his chance to turn a few laps around the famed Brickyard.

Career breaks sometimes come in the most unexpected places. When Bonnett looked through his helmet to his left, he saw a track official walking toward him.

"Mr. Bonnett, you have a very important phone call," the official said.

Bonnett looked surprised and said, "I'm sort of busy right now. Who is it?"

The official said, "Some guy named Glen Wood."

Bonnett thought to himself, "What does Glen Wood want to talk to me about?"

Bonnett worked his way out of the cockpit and ran to the telephone. Wood, leader of the famed Wood Brothers NASCAR Winston Cup team, promptly offered Bonnett one of the premier rides of the time, available because the Woods and driver David Pearson had mutually parted company. Bonnett accepted the ride, leaving the Indy car sitting in line for practice without a driver.

Bonnett had earned that now-historic phone call. For him, as with many racers, the road to the top had been a long, hard struggle. He was a professional pipe fitter, an occupation that helped finance his first love, racing. Bonnett continued to race with passion until his death in 1994.

Racing automobiles was the way he lived, and the way he died.

The Alabama native lived in Hueytown, a quiet community whose most popular resident was stock car great Bobby Allison. Bonnett raced on short tracks around Birmingham and Montgomery, his first start coming on April 12, 1969, in the Cadet Division. He was drawn to Allison's shop like a tack to a magnet, seizing the opportunity to call on one of the best racing instructors available—right in his back yard.

Bonnett drove in a few Winston Cup races in 1974, but he spent most of his time working on Allison's cars. He worked so hard and long it prompted Allison to pay Bonnett "wages" in the form of a car to race at Talladega Superspeedway in 1975.

Sporadic starts came the next year, but Bonnett didn't attract much attention until he

Neil Bonnett carries the Wood Brothers' colors again in 1982 with the down-sized Ford Thunderbirds. His only win that year came in the World 600 at Charlotte.

Under Junior Johnson's direction, Bonnett's finishes at the front became more consistent. Here, he is shown en route to a fourth place finish at North Wilkesboro (North Carolina) Speedway in 1984.

qualified Allison's Mercury for the pole position at Richmond, Virginia, in March of 1976. Allison had suffered a frightening crash at Rockingham, North Carolina, the week before and had been out of the hospital less than four days when Bonnett sped to the top of the Richmond grid. In July of 1976, he repeated the feat at Nashville, Tennessee, after Allison was injured in a short track event at Elko, Minnesota.

In 1977, Bonnett finally secured the first-class ride he longed for by joining owner Nord Krauskopf. Bonnett quickly proved he could win races. Later, a few more victories came with owner Jim Stacy.

Which brought Bonnett to the call he received from Wood while sitting in an Indy car in 1979. After Bonnett hung up the phone, he had a quick conversation with Hodgdon. The two men boarded a jet to Virginia to iron out the details.

That complete, Bonnett spent four seasons with the Woods, producing nine victories. Theirs was one of the closest relationships between driver and team stock car racing had ever seen.

As his career evolved, Bonnett enjoyed success with team owners Butch Mock and Bob Rahilly in 1983. He wheeled Chevrolets for Junior Johnson from 1984 through 1986 and rejoined Mock and Rahilly in 1987, the season in which he suffered a severely broken leg while racing at Charlotte Motor Speedway.

Back with Mock and Rahilly in 1988, he rebounded from his injury to record two emotion-charged victories.

The next year, he rejoined the Wood Brothers.

In 1990, a serious accident at Darlington, South Carolina, left Bonnett reeling from

injuries that included a broken sternum and a concussion severe enough to cause amnesia.

Such a severe crash could easily have ended his driving career. Unfortunately, that was not to be.

Bonnett eventually returned to the tracks to test for driver Dale Earnhardt and team owner Richard Childress. Away from the track, his talents as a television broadcaster became widely recognized. He was considered one of the best television commentators because of his infectious personality and ability to convey racing information in terms that fans could understand. Realizing that, several friends and members of the media tried to talk him out of a return to the driver's seat.

They failed to convince him to stay away.

On February 11, 1994, Bonnett was scheduled to attempt to qualify a Chevrolet owned by James Finch for the Daytona 500, but struck the fourth turn wall head-on at 190 miles per hour during the first practice session of the season. He died at 1:17 P.M., but official word didn't come until 5:25 P.M., nearly five hours after the crash.

"Neil was a great competitor and a great friend," said Allison after Bonnett's death. "He was determined to make his mark and did so at times with limited equipment. He died doing exactly what he wanted to do. It's hard to argue with that."

Bonnett is survived by his wife, Susan, a son, David, and a daughter, Kristen.

# HENRY NEIL "SOAPY" CASTLES 1934-

When Henry Neil "Soapy" Castles began delivering newspapers to Buddy Shuman's garage, he never dreamed he would one day fill the headlines of the sports pages.

Castles loved anything with wheels. As partial payment for sweeping floors and keeping the shop organized, Castles was given a brand new soapbox derby racer that Shuman's shop workers built for him; thus, the name "Soapy" Castles was born. For a couple of summers, Castles drove his soapbox racer in several events. All the while, he found ways to make his wheels go faster and faster.

He then moved into Midget car racing with backing from fellow Charlotte, North Carolinian Bob Harkey. While Castles gravitated toward the Modifieds, Sportsman, and the NASCAR Convertible division, Harkey went north and began running Sprint cars and Indy cars.

Castles ran his first NASCAR event at the Columbia (South Carolina) Speedway on June 20, 1957. At about the same time, Castles' driving abilities netted him a membership in the Screen Actors' Guild. Castles, Lee Petty, and Speedy Thompson were hired to drive stock cars for a scene in a television series that starred James Whitmore. In the scene, a Californian stuntman was supposed to crash a stock car. The stuntman never made it to Hillsboro, North Carolina, where the scene was filmed. Disgusted with waiting and wanting to go home for Thanksgiving, Castles offered do the stunt—rolling a car down a hill—if the director would just shoot the shot and give him his money.

In order to perform the stunt, Castles had to sign a nine-page document that allowed him to become a member of the Screen Actors' Guild. In the scene, Castles was to drive a race car and allow Lee Petty to shove him into the wall. When Petty asked him how he wanted to work the scene, Castles sent word back through Richard Petty that as many times as Lee Petty

had raced, if he didn't know how to slam someone into the wall by now, Castles wasn't going to tell him. The scene went off without a hitch. Castles rolled the car 14 times across a thicket and creek.

The stunt was the beginning of Castles' long Hollywood career. He worked with Rory Calhoun in *Thunder in Carolina* and Elvis Presley in *Speedway*. Castles also worked on *Greased Lightning* (1977), which was the Wendell Scott Story, and *Six Pack* (1982), Castles' last racing film. He has worked in several movies of the week and on *Matlock*, a popular weekly television series starring Andy Griffith.

During his NASCAR Winston Cup driving career, Castles entered 280 events with about 176 of them top-10 finishes, including around

Castles takes to the high banks of Daytona 500 of 1970. He finished 12th.

50 finishes in the top 5 with about 18 team owners, including himself. All told, his efforts generated $230,000 in winnings.

Through it all, Castles contributed a great deal to NASCAR Winston Cup racing. Even though his driving career ended in 1976 without a Winston Cup victory, his name is still widely recognized by his fans.

His only victory came at Greenville, South Carolina, on April 1, 1972, in a NASCAR Grand National East event. He led for several laps in his 1971 Dodge and won the race on the last lap over Lee Roy Yarbrough, David Pearson, and Elmo Langley.

Soapy Castles next to his 1969 Dodge Daytona at the Daytona 500 in 1970.

When the windshield of his racer caved in from flying debris at Charlotte in the mid-1960s, Castles wrapped his face, removed the glass, and continued on.

Castles uses a special shoulder harness connected to his helmet to keep the G-forces manageable at Bristol (Tennessee) Motor Speedway.

One of the tricks of the trade was to use baby powder to help make the waxed paint schemes glide even better through the wind. Castles claimed he could gain an extra mile per hour in qualifying.

# DALE EARNHARDT 1951-

From his earliest recollections, Dale Earnhardt has known nothing but the sound of race engines and the glory they have brought him. Whether it was tricycles in the driveway of the family home, bicycles on the sidewalks of Kannapolis, North Carolina, or race cars at Metrolina (North Carolina) Speedway, Savannah (Georgia) Speedway, or Hickory (North Carolina) Speedway, he made his presence known week after week, usually by besting all challengers.

His "Intimidator, man in black" image has shaken some of the best drivers in the business. The black-and-silver number three Chevrolet is one of the most feared images to appear in a NASCAR driver's rearview mirror.

His quiet nature adds all the more to his image, as it is translated into someone cocky, overly confident, and virtually untouchable. Nothing could be further from the truth. He is warm and personable to those who know him but possesses a competitive spirit that puts him in a league of his own.

The lavish lifestyle Earnhardt enjoys today was only a distant dream during the early years of his Winston Cup career. The son of 1956 Sportsman champion Ralph Earnhardt, he counted heavily on his father's expertise to help build his fledgling career. Father and son were distant at times, especially when the younger elected to quit school in the ninth grade to devote his every breath to racing. The decision nearly divided them, but eventually both were able to patch their differences. Their time working as a team was, however, running out.

While Ralph built his engines, Dale handled the chassis work. During his second year of driving, he won 26 races and looked to be on his way. There were even more wins his third year.

Suddenly, the unthinkable happened.

The senior Earnhardt died of a massive heart attack at age 45, leaving behind little hope of success and little direction to follow. His 19-year-old son simply didn't know where to turn.

The next year, 1974, was the worst year of Earnhardt's life. Money was tight, often not enough to keep food in the kitchen cabinets while he and his wife and two children moved from run-down mobile home to cheap apartment. He worked installing insulation, rebuilding car engines, anything that would put numbers in his wallet other than those stamped on his driver's license.

Work was impossible to find in the mill town where he lived. After moving from temporary job to temporary job, Earnhardt worked as a subcontractor with the Boilermaker's Union in the North Carolina coastal town of New Bern. He spent eight long days and nights, including Christmas day, helping to make welding repairs to machinery in a paper mill, hating every minute.

When money could be saved for parts, he raced the Camaro his father once campaigned, and took on any other rides he could muster. By 1974, he quit the work force and went racing

---

He is warm and personable to those who know him but possesses a competitive spirit that puts him in a league of his own.

---

full time. He lost his first wife to divorce, married again, divorced again, and continued to starve.

On a dozen or so occasions, the Winston Cup circuit came his way with team owners Ed Negre, Will Cronkite, Henley Gray, and Johnny Ray. Finishes were mediocre, to say the least, but his worst scare came while driving Ray's Ford at Atlanta on November 7, 1976. On lap 260 of the 328-lap event, Earnhardt and driver Dick Brooks collided, sending Earnhardt into a frightening end-over-end spill. Miraculously, he suffered only minor injuries, but the violence of the wreck could never be forgotten.

By 1978, Earnhardt was nursing his efforts on the short tracks while continuing to flirt with the Winston Cup circuit. He would scrape money to buy parts, often going to the shops of Rod Osterlund, Digard Racing and its owners Bill and Jim Gardner, or Junior Johnson.

During visits to Osterlund's impressive facility, Earnhardt would strike up conversations with Roland Wlodyka, Osterlund's general manager of racing operations. Persistence with both Osterlund and Wlodyka paid off, as Earnhardt was given a second car to drive behind the team's regular driver, Dave Marcis, at Atlanta in the season finale. Surprising everyone except himself, he finished fourth, one lap down.

Osterlund called Earnhardt in late December 1978 and offered him the role as his full-time chauffeur. The next season, Earnhardt won at Bristol, Tennessee, en route to capturing the Rookie of the Year honors. He paid Osterlund further for his faith in him by giving the California businessman his first and only Winston Cup championship in 1980. Throughout the sport's 50-year history, he is the only man to win those honors back to back.

By mid-season 1981, Osterlund sold his team unexpectedly to coal magnate J. D. Stacy without consulting with his driver or crew, a move that devastated Earnhardt.

Earnhardt quit the team in May of that year to take a ride vacated by Richard Childress, a long-time campaigner who got close to victory in the Winston Cup but never found that elusive win.

Earnhardt and Childress showed promise, but the latter turned Earnhardt away, reasoning that his talent outweighed the team's equipment. Two seasons with Bud Moore and his Fords provided a few wins, but by 1984, Earnhardt signed with Childress again. The combination was one of the most successful unions in NASCAR history. They amassed a mind-boggling six Winston Cup championships (Earnhardt won one other with Rod Osterlund), 61 wins, 17 pole positions, and $26 million in race winnings with Childress and $28 million overall.

On three occasions during his career, injury came to him. During his rookie season in 1979, he flipped his Chevrolet at Pocono, suffering cuts, bruises, and two broken collerbones. At Pocono three years later, Earnhardt broke his left knee cap. In 1996, he suffered a cracked sternum and broken shoulder blade, ending his bid for an eighth championship.

"Dale Earnhardt is a great individual and a great competitor," says Childress. "I knew firsthand when I raced against him in the 1970s the talent he possessed. Just like his father, Ralph, he's always had that deep determination to be a champion. His focus on winning has always impressed me.

"To both of us, NASCAR racing has been our lives and our livelihood. Early on, we won races together because we had to win. The alternative to that was not being able to survive in the sport.

"We've enjoyed a tremendous amount of success together over the years, all from Dale's masterful job of driving race cars and the talented people who built him winning equipment. I'm proud to be associated with him."

Dale Earnhardt enjoying a win of "The Winston Select." This race is a special event held a week before the Coca-Cola 600. He won $222,500 in earnings.

Earnhardt in 1974.

Ralph Earnhardt (Dale's father) died in 1973 of a massive heart attack. This picture was taken at the Charlotte Fairgrounds a few years before his death.

The start of the Atlanta Journal 500 on November 6, 1983. Earnhardt started his Bud Moore Ford in the front row alongside Tim Richmond. Earnhardt finished 33rd.

left: Earnhardt and his long hair in the mid-1980s.

Earnhardt relaxing at the lake between races.

Earnhardt blasts through traffic on his way to winning the Hanes 500 at Martinsville, Virginia, on April 28, 1991.

Earnhardt waiting to go out for a few laps at Charlotte in October 1995.

right: Earnhardt at Daytona in February 1995.

# BILL ELLIOTT 1955-

When Bill Elliott was a young man looking to kill time at his Cumming, Georgia, home, cars from his father's junkyard drew the most of he and his brothers' time and attention.

Elliott and his brothers, Ernie and Dan, picked their rides from the lot and got them running. They then laid out a track around the yard—a rusted Oldsmobile was the inside of turn one, an old Ford truck marked turn two, an oak tree maybe for turn three, and so forth. Bill usually bested his older brothers, but the racing lit all the boys up with ear-to-ear smiles. The boys of George and Mildred Elliott had found their calling.

When Winston Cup events came to Atlanta Motor Speedway, the Elliotts were usually there in force, in the infield or in the stands, dreaming of racing against the Pearsons, the Pettys, and the Allisons. With little money to speak of, it was just that back then—a dream. The only way for Bill to cut his racing teeth was on back roads and an occasional pasture track that sprang up among the moonshiners who lived in the north Georgia mountains.

The racing bug got serious among the boys and there was no question Bill was the family's driver. George Elliott owned race cars on a local level and on occasion fielded a car at Daytona. Young Bill would warm them up at places like Woodstock, Rome, and Macon in Georgia and Chattanooga, Tennessee, then turned the wheel over to someone else. By the time he turned 16, he was racing himself.

Ernie's talents fell within the realm of engines while Dan specialized in race car building and preparation. The fledgling race team spent summer weekends competing on small dirt tracks. George Elliott owned a building supply outlet, as well as a few other small businesses and later a Ford dealership. He acted as their early sponsor and financier.

After some strong persuasion from all three brothers, George finally agreed to finance a Winston Cup effort. The Elliott team first ran a Winston Cup race on February 29, 1976, at Rockingham, North Carolina. Bill finally made his debut in NASCAR's elite circle, finishing 33rd with $640 of prize money in his pocket. The team raced a beat-up old Ford Torino purchased from Bobby Allison. The car had already seen its share of better days. Still, the

Bill Elliott sports a special black uniform to match the black Ford known as the "Batmobile" he drove in The Winston at Charlotte in May 1995.

> The only way for Bill to cut his racing teeth was on back roads and an occasional pasture track that sprang up among the moonshiners who lived in the north Georgia mountains.

boys felt they were rich with the pot of gold they collected.

More cars followed, including a Mercury bought from Roger Penske. In five years of limited Winston Cup appearances, the Elliotts managed to exhaust their budget for a few impressive runs, but did not have enough success to keep the team operating. Then came Harry Melling, a businessman from Jackson, Michigan, who offered limited sponsorship to various teams, including Benny Parsons while he was with Bud Moore's operation. Melling gave Elliott backing for one race in 1981. The talent of the Elliott brothers was obvious and too good to pass up.

Understanding the Elliotts' plight, Melling bought the team by the end of the 1981 season. By 1983, Elliott was driving the entire schedule for the first time in his career. In the last race of the season at Riverside, California, that first victory finally came in young Elliott's 117th start.

Three victories came in 1984 to help set the stage for the incredible 1985 season. It was the year Elliott and Company had arrived. Bill won 11 races in 28 starts, starting his assault by dominating the Daytona 500. He won at Atlanta and Darlington, and overwhelmed the competition at Talladega in May, winning the pole position with a speed of 202.398 miles per hour. He broke an oil line during the race, but made up 5 miles under green conditions by turning lap after lap at more than 205 miles per hour, regaining the lost deficit to win the race.

The come-from-behind victory at Talladega was his second win of the four major NASCAR events. To win three meant he would be awarded an incredible $1 million bonus from R. J. Reynolds, the series sponsor.

Elliott suffered brake problems at the next $1 million-eligible event at Charlotte, but came back at Darlington to win the prestigious Southern 500 and the bonus. No other driver has captured the bonus since Elliott accomplished the feat in its inaugural year.

Elliott turned the fastest time in a stock car at 212.809 in August 1987 at Talladega and was crowned Winston Cup champion in 1988. Since that first start in 1976, Elliott has logged 40 career victories and 48 pole positions.

In 1996, Elliott suffered a severely broken leg near his right hip at Talladega, Alabama. Before season's end, he was back in a stock car. In 1997, he was back on the full schedule, looking for more success.

On July 2, 1988, Elliott adds another win to his Daytona list.

In tight quarters at Martinsville, Virginia, in 1991, Elliott searches for an advantage.

Elliott shares a light moment with Dale Jarrett at Rockingham, North Carolina, in 1995.

On his way to winning the Winston Million, a special non-points bonus for victories at Daytona, Charlotte, and Darlington in the same year, Elliott stops for fuel and tires at the Darlington race in 1985. Elliott won 11 races that year but was edged out for the championship by Darrell Waltrip.

Elliott finds a new use for his winner's trophy after his win at Atlanta on March 17, 1985.

# TIM FLOCK 1924-

At five years of age, the brilliant blue eyes of Julius Timothy Flock had seen plenty of empty dinner tables. The Flock family, like thousands of others, struggled to put something, anything, worth eating on the table during the Great Depression.

During those hard times, honest work and decent wages became scarce in the Flock's hometown of Fort Payne, Alabama. As with the rest of the country, soup lines served the poor and affluent alike. Survival was the only thing on everyone's minds.

While sermons from the pulpit kept spirits of the God-fearing from sinking, spirits of homegrown corn liquor kept their church doors open. In those difficult days, gainful employment included backwoods bootlegging.

Tim's mother, Maudi Josie Williams Flock, needed something to supplement her modest wages earned in a hosiery mill. Her husband, Lee Preston Flock, died in 1925, and hauling liquor seemed to be the answer to feeding her 10 children. Tim's older brothers, Carl, Bob, and Fonty, joined their uncle, Peachtree Williams, in the Atlanta whiskey trade. Two runs a day to Dahlonega, Georgia, netted them $200 a week, a small fortune in those days.

Both Bob and Fonty ran moonshine, while young Tim went along for the ride from time to time. By the 1930s, the older brothers engaged in some unorganized modified racing among the Atlanta whiskey runners.

Bets were placed on the barrel head as to which car was the fastest. In a cow pasture in Stockbridge, Georgia, in 1934, 30 or so bootleggers raced several laps, and as many as 300 spectators would show up to watch. Little did they know they were laying the foundation for a very popular, very lucrative professional sport.

Tim went there to watch as well and found his life's calling. But he didn't get to drive until 1947 at North Wilkesboro, North Carolina. On October 23 of that year, Tim won his first race at Lakewood Speedway in Atlanta. Flock went on to win 39 more races in 189 starts and 39 pole positions.

Flock drove for such car owners as Buddy Elliott, Ted Chester, and Bill Stroppe, to name a few. Even though he won 16 races and the 1952 championship with Chester, his greatest

Flock in his 1939 Ford Coupe in about 1948 at a track near Lexington, North Carolina.

Flock describes himself as the most disqualified driver in history. He and Bill France, the founder of the most successful stock car sanction in the world, had many heated battles.

success came with Carl Kiekhaefer, the inventor of Mercury Marine Outboard Motors. Flock and Kiekhaefer won 21 races together, 18 of which came in 1955, the year of Flock's second national championship.

While with Chester, Flock carried a rhesus monkey named "Jocko" with him in as many as 13 races. On May 30, 1953, the monkey got loose from his special seat and pulled a chain to a trapdoor used to check the tire wear of the right front. Getting too close, the monkey's head was sanded by the tire, causing him to run around the cockpit wildly. As a result, Flock had to pit, relegating himself to third instead of first.

Flock describes himself as the most disqualified driver in history. He and Bill France, the founder of the most successful stock car sanction in the world, had many heated battles. Flock was initially banned from competition for life in 1961 for attempting to unionize the drivers. In 1965, both he and Curtis Turner, the principal organizer, were reinstated. Flock never again raced in a NASCAR-sanctioned event.

For many years after he left the driver's seat, Flock worked with the Charlotte (North Carolina) Motor Speedway. Today he enjoys retirement in his Charlotte home and continues to follow NASCAR racing.

In May 1991, Flock entered a special non-points event called the Winston Legends Race, hosted by R. J. Reynolds Tobacco Company. That was his last stock car race as a driver.

Tim Flock was program director for the Charlotte Motor Speedway in 1960. *Charlotte Motor Speedway*

# BILL FRANCE, SR. 1909-1992

It's often been said that William Henry Getty France knew how to perform miracles. He made things happen out of sheer determination and an overwhelming talent for salesmanship.

France was born in Washington, D.C., on September 20, 1909, and by his 17th birthday, was making money turning wrenches on passenger cars at a local Buick dealership. He traveled north to Laurel, Maryland, to watch a car race held on a board track called Baltimore-Washington Speedway. That fateful day in 1926 changed the face of automobile racing forever.

France worked to support his family by day and built a race car at night. He then competed on tracks in the Washington, Maryland, and Virginia area when time permitted. Times were lean, however, so France, his wife, Anne, and son, Bill Jr., packed their belongings and headed south to Miami in pursuit of a better financial future.

France withdrew his total savings of $75 from his Washington bank account and purchased $50 worth of tools to make repairs for stranded motorists along the way.

A stop in Daytona Beach to see where land speed records were set curtailed the trip to Miami. The Frances rented an apartment, and Bill made a living doing auto repair work. And, as he did during the days up north, France raced, this time in several events on the Daytona sand.

What started as a dream roughly drawn out on a pad of paper from behind a desk at his service station became a phenomenon in the stock car racing world.

On December 14, 1947, France met with 35 businessmen from around the country at the famed Streamline Hotel (now used as a home for the elderly). In the room that Sunday was a filling-station operator, a local race driver, a motorcycle dealer, a garage operator, a turnip farmer, a race-track promoter, a moonshiner or two, and a few assorted hustlers, among others.

By late afternoon, France and his makeshift advisory board had a tentative plan on paper to create the most successful governing body of stock car racing in the history of motorsports. It was named the National Association for Stock Car Automobile Racing.

NASCAR.

France soon found he had to rule his fledgling organization with an iron fist. For every success "Big Bill" enjoyed, there were many headaches to endure. Innovative competitors had to be kept within the rules,

Bill France, Sr., stands beside the car he drove at Talladega in 1969 in hopes of holding off the PDA strike at his new superspeedway.

Richard Brickhouse emerged victorious in the controversial Talladega 500 of 1969. Alongside is South Carolina Congressman Mendell Rivers and France who, like Brickhouse, had won the day.

**What started as a dream roughly drawn out on a pad of paper from behind a desk at his service station became a phenomenon in the stock car racing world.**

money was needed to pay purses with gate sales that didn't always cover the cost, the attempt to unionize the drivers was repelled, inclement weather was always a threat, and creditors demanding a declaration of bankruptcy needed to be satisfied.

Once, reportedly, while France was negotiating for new money with bank executives in the living room of the family home, Annie B. France, the stellar corporate business manager, was negotiating with creditors on past-due accounts at the France filling station.

As finances became more stable, France co-owned and nurtured Martinsville (Virginia) Speedway and Bowman-Gray Stadium in Winston-Salem, North Carolina. He built Daytona International Speedway in 1959 and Alabama International Motor Speedway, known today as Talladega Superspeedway, 10 years later. During the inaugural Talladega race on September 14, 1969, France saw many of his star drivers walk away for fear that tires wouldn't hold up at

high speeds. At 60 years of age, France drove a Ford Torino at 175 miles per hour to prove the tires were safe.

France vowed to hold a race, even if the members of the Professional Drivers Association (PDA) turned their backs on him. He allowed drivers from the Grand American ranks to fill the field of 36 cars.

Richard Brickhouse of Rocky Point, North Carolina, won the race over Jim Vandiver and Ramo Stott. Because he didn't boycott with his fellow drivers, many have theorized Brickhouse was blackballed for winning the race.

With the PDA incident finally behind him, France had survived one of stock car racing's darkest days.

Slowly and deliberately, France nurtured his dream from a struggling regional sport that received little press to the premier form of auto racing in the world, with Bill Jr. taking the helm in 1972.

France died on June 7, 1992, of complications from a long bout with Alzheimer's disease. At his death, he did not realize the fortunes he brought to the sport and the joy he brought to millions of motorsports enthusiasts around the world.

# JEFF GORDON 1971-

When Jeff Gordon was on stage in New York to accept the NASCAR Winston Cup championship in 1995, he looked as though he should have been serving hamburger combo meals rather than serving notice he was to become the next phenomenon in stock car racing. He was the sport's version of golf's Tiger Woods. Jeff Gordon quickly became a household name, known to both grizzled longtime fans and preschool children.

Although only in his fifth year of Winston Cup racing, Gordon was every bit the crafty veteran twice his age. Not since Richard Petty entered into NASCAR in 1958 has a driver shown such overwhelming promise. He was talented behind the wheel, articulate, and handsome. Gordon is a public relations dream, the perfect role model capable of reaching beyond the stereotypical fan and into the national limelight.

The Vallejo, California, native began his racing career at age 5 in quarter midgets and go-carts. By his 10th birthday, he was already twice a national champion. With his talent, the sky was the limit.

In 1984, John Bickford, Gordon's stepfather, moved his family to Indiana, a hotbed for drivers looking for experience and national exposure, to take advantage of his potential.

Other prestigious awards and records fell to Gordon like tipping dominos. In both 1979 and 1981, he won quarter midget championships. In 1990, he was crowned the USAC Midget champion. A year later, he was the 1991 USAC Silver Crown champion. There was little else to conquer where open wheel short-track racing was concerned. Gordon logged more than 500 victories. He was the hottest sprint car driver in America.

Gordon garnered several offers from various forms of auto racing while still a teenager. One such offer came from former Formula One world champion Jackie Stewart, who was searching for a young hot shoe to drive road courses for his team in Europe. Other offers came from Indy car teams looking for a new star.

Gordon did his homework. He studied all he could and then decided to pursue stock car racing. He turned laps at Martinsville (Virginia) Speedway in a Busch Series Pontiac owned by businessman Hugh Connerty. The test session went well, and Gordon found his home in motorsports.

The accolades continued to come.

In 1991, his first year in the Busch Series

Around the turn at Martinsville, Virginia, in 1996, Jeff Gordon is in his customary position—out front.

> Gordon is a public relations dream, the perfect role model capable of reaching beyond the stereotypical fan and into the national limelight.

division, Gordon won Rookie of the Year honors. In 1992, he won 11 Busch Series pole positions and scored three victories.

Gordon debuted in Winston Cup competition at the final event of the 1992 Winston Cup season. He was under 21 years of age and had to get written permission from his parents to compete. He finished unremarkably, in 31st place, but his career soon took off.

Rookie of the Year honors in the Winston Cup ranks followed in 1993, as well as the distinction of becoming the youngest driver to win a 125-mile qualifying race at Daytona International Speedway. He was the first rookie to do so since Johnny Rutherford in 1963.

By 1994, Gordon was becoming a household name. He started his season by winning the Busch Clash as well as The Winston at Charlotte Motor Speedway, a special nonpoints event. He captured his first Winston Cup win at the Coca-

Cola 600 at Charlotte Motor Speedway in May. He capped that win with a victory in the prestigious Brickyard 400 at Indianapolis Motor Speedway in August, making him the first stock car driver to grace Indy's coveted victory circle.

By the end of 1995, Gordon had accomplished the unthinkable by winning his first Winston Cup championship over the likes of Dale Earnhardt, Terry Labonte, and Rusty Wallace. He was in only his third full season. He became the youngest Winston Cup champion in the modern era (since 1972) and the second youngest overall (1950 NASCAR champion Bill Rexford was only a few months younger).

In 1997, Gordon won his second career NASCAR Winston Cup championship and has collected $15 million in winnings.

"When he came over to talk to me that first time, he still had that little mustache and he didn't look as big as my daughter," Rick Hendrick, Gordon's team owner, once said. "I said to him, 'God, you can't be old enough to drive one of these cars.' I was really excited because here was this guy that had talent, good looks, and youth. He had it all."

Jeff Gordon at the Pepsi 400 held at Daytona in 1995. He started third and finished first.

# JOHN HOLMAN 1918-1976 RALPH MOODY 1918-

The combination of John Holman and Ralph Moody was one of the most powerful unions in motorsports history. Despite different backgrounds and an often stormy relationship, the two men brought innovations to the track that became NASCAR standards still in use today, not to mention running one of the highest-profile race teams in NASCAR history.

First, in order to look at Holman-Moody's rich contribution to stock car racing, one must look into Ford Motor Company's history with stock cars.

The Ford brass searched for a way to enter NASCAR racing almost out of necessity, as Chevrolet was winning races and getting the attention of the fans with regularity. To combat their competitor on the racetrack and Chevrolet's full-page newspaper ads that bragged about their on-track success, Ford executive Bill Benton took driver Buddy Shuman to Detroit to talk to design engineers about what would make a winner on the track. Shuman's comments weren't met with optimism.

Benton talked the engineers into building two Fords for the 1955 Southern 500 at Darlington, South Carolina. Drivers Curtis Turner and Joe Weatherly were tapped as the cars' drivers. Neither finished the race, while Chevrolet driver Herb Thomas logged his third Southern 500 win. Ford was scrambling for answers. Sales at the marketplace were dropping. Ford's biggest problem was an inferior product to the Chevrolet, as the General Motors car make was a rolling test bed for its passenger cars. What was learned on the racetrack was eventually put into the car designs. Ford wasn't following suit and wouldn't for several years.

Soon after, Pete DePaolo, a former Indianapolis 500 champion, was hired to field the Ford race teams through his automotive engineering firm. Problems soon surfaced twofold. Having the operation some 3,000 miles away in California wasn't sound, both economically or logistically. Second, DePaolo didn't possess the administrative ability to field such a huge operation. To answer that problem in part, Shuman was hired as DePaolo's manager on the East Coast. Shuman hired John Holman, a truck driver with great organizational skills, as his assistant.

Shuman died in a hotel fire on November 13, 1955, in Hickory, North Carolina, after taking the Fords of Turner and Weatherly there for a race. Red Vogt, a master mechanic, replaced Shuman, but the union with Vogt and Holman didn't last.

On May 24, 1956, while working on a race car, Holman and Vogt engaged in some heated words, causing Vogt to quit on the spot. After a phone call was placed to DePaolo and a complaint about Holman was registered, Vogt knew exactly where he stood. Soon after, Holman then began to head the eastern racing operation for Ford.

Holman was at Lehi, Arkansas, on June 10, 1956, when driver Ralph Moody wheeled a DePaolo Ford to a second-place finish behind Jim Paschal's Mercury. Holman protested the finish and finally had the decision reversed to give Moody the win after much persuasion and countless checks of the scorecards.

Alliances were being formed between driver and car maker. Ford's drivers were Fireball Roberts and Marvin Panch. The trump card was Ford's hiring of Smokey Yunick, a crack mechanic who had led Thomas to much success. He would be Ford's tool to gain ground on Chevrolet.

In January 1957, Jacques Passino joined Ford in its sales promotion office and later

---

## Aside from having a stellar reputation for building cars, Holman-Moody was also a powerhouse at fielding them.

---

became head of Ford's racing operation. He was tough but got the desired results.

On June 6 of that year, the Automobile Manufacturer's Association banned participation in auto racing. The last factory-backed race came on June 1 at Lancaster, South Carolina, with Paul Goldsmith winning in Yunick's Ford. When the race was over, each Ford driver was given his two race cars, a tow truck, and a supply of parts as a bonus for his efforts.

Thus came the birth of Holman-Moody. With the ban, Ford pulled all factory support. Holman went to Passino with a bid to buy all remaining equipment. Holman-Moody paid $12,000 for an enormous amount of race cars and equipment. Their operation made a nice profit over the next few years by selling the stockpile accumulated, as well as the manufacturing of new racing chassis for anyone who wanted them.

Eventually, the Holman-Moody operation employed 325 workers building turn-key race cars to anyone with the money to purchase them. A rolling racer of the early to mid-1960s could be bought for around

$5,000. In assembly-line fashion, cars were completed from start to finish and carried a reputation as being the best.

Aside from having a stellar reputation for building cars, Holman-Moody was also a powerhouse at fielding them. Aside from Turner, Weatherly, and Roberts, drivers Fred Lorenzen, Dick Hutcherson, Bobby Allison, Donnie Allison, David Pearson, Cale Yarborough, Benny Parsons, Jimmy Clark, Mario Andretti, and Bobby Unser, to name a few, drove Holman-Moody cars at some point during their careers. Of those drivers, Pearson won the Winston Cup (then Grand National) championship in 1968 and 1969. The last Holman-Moody car to be fielded in NASCAR competition came on January 21, 1973, at Riverside, California, with Unser behind the wheel. Not long after, the majority of the stock car equipment was sold at auction. Another auction was held in the early 1980s.

Holman-Moody continues today under the direction of Lee Holman, son of the late John Holman. The company produces the GT40 Mark II for Vintage Car races. Holman Automotive does camshaft and engine work for the Wood Brothers and has for several decades through the talents of Tommy Turner.

With Holman's organizational flair and Moody's wizardry with chassis preparation, the union was quite successful. More than once, however, their personalities clashed, causing strife that lasted until Holman's death on December 27, 1976. Ironically, Holman suffered a heart attack while driving a truck during the testing of a new truck part he was set to patent.

Moody continues to reside in Charlotte, North Carolina, and has acted as a consultant for several race teams over the years.

"The biggest thing Holman-Moody should be remembered for is something that few people give the company credit for," says Lee Holman. "Without the standardization of the chassis designs, suspension, and the items that Dad should have patented but didn't, NASCAR simply wouldn't exist. It was the Holman-Moody chassis, roof suspension, and full-floating rear end, the check valve for the fuel system, that allowed the NASCAR cars to be dependable and safe and allowed enough of the same pieces to be used on identical cars, even though they were Fords or Chevys or whatever. By standardizing the cost of all that, it brought the cost to the individual racer down where it was affordable.

"Today, NASCAR is still using any number of items that were designed by Holman and Moody."

*Ralph Moody (left) and John Holman put together one of stock car racing's most powerful unions, building race-ready cars and fielding a formidable team until 1973.*

Left to right, Moody and Waddell Wilson.

Left to right, Moody, Eddie Pagan, Mario Andretti, and Jake Elder.

Tim Flock (300) battles with Moody (12).

Pictured at the Daytona 500 in the late 1960s are the crewmen for Fred Lorenzen, from left to right, Jack Sullivan, Fred McCall, and Moody.

left: Holman and Moody formed their relationship working for the early factory Ford team in the 1950s. The pair got started officially when they bought the remnants of Ford's factory race team in 1957.

Holman, shown here talking with Junior Johnson, suffered a fatal heart attack in 1976.

# ERNIE IRVAN 1959-

Ernie Irvan's first job in NASCAR was welding new steel seating at Charlotte Motor Speedway. On occasion, he would break from his work to look out onto the track and dream of a Winston Cup career of his own.

A native of Salinas, California, a small town just south of San Diego, Irvan first began driving stock cars at Stockton Speedway in California and won the track championship in 1977. On several occasions, he would visit the now-defunct Ontario (California) Motor Speedway when the Winston Cup tour visited the super-speedway each year.

Irvan made the move to the East Coast by 1984 and worked a variety of jobs, including construction, to make ends meet. His California racing success helped land him a ride at the Concord (North Carolina) Speedway. By the mid-1980s, Irvan had secured another track championship.

In 1987, Irvan was given his first Winston Cup ride at Richmond, Virginia, on September 13 with team owner Marc Reno. After only 35 laps, Irvan pulled in with overheating problems. His next start came at Charlotte, again in Reno's Chevrolet, with sponsorship provided by Dale Earnhardt's car dealership. An impressive top-10 finish in his second outing was quickly noticed.

Irvan joined D. K. Ulrich and Junie Donlavey for 60 events into 1990. Then team owner Larry McClure of Morgan-McClure Racing offered him a full-time position in the team's potent Chevrolets. His first Winston Cup victory came on August 25, 1990, at Bristol, Tennessee. Six more victories came through the midway point of 1993, including a Daytona 500 victory in 1991.

Those wins came amid harsh criticism from fellow drivers about what they perceived to be Irvan's careless driving style. Many blamed Irvan for a multicar accident at Talladega Superspeedway in Alabama on May 6 that caused Kyle Petty to suffer a severely broken leg. Irvan made a public apology for that incident.

When Robert Yates driver Davey Allison died in a helicopter crash at Talladega on July 13, 1993, Irvan settled his contract with McClure and was released to drive for Robert Yates Racing. Going into Michigan International Speedway in August 1994, Irvan trailed Dale Earnhardt by 27 points and was a strong contender to win the Winston Cup championship. He won three races in 20 starts leading to the Michigan event.

While at Michigan on August 20, Irvan was critically injured in a crash that occurred during an early morning practice session. He suffered severe head injuries as well as collapsed lungs, internal bleeding, and swelling of the brain stem. Doctors gave him only a 10 percent chance of survival.

Irvan spent several days barely hanging on to life. After a lengthy hospital stay, he made a miraculous recovery. Other than difficulties with his left eye, Irvan was back. With the use of an eye patch, Irvan was granted permission to test at Darlington, South Carolina, 14 months after the crash.

In his first three outings in 1995, he was competitive, finishing sixth at North Wilkes-boro, North Carolina, and seventh at Atlanta, Georgia. In 1996, Irvan won races at Loudon, New Hampshire, and Richmond, Virginia. That year, he logged 16 top 10s and 12 top 5s to finish 10th in the Winston Cup point standings.

In 1997, Irvan won at Michigan Speedway, the site of his horrific crash.

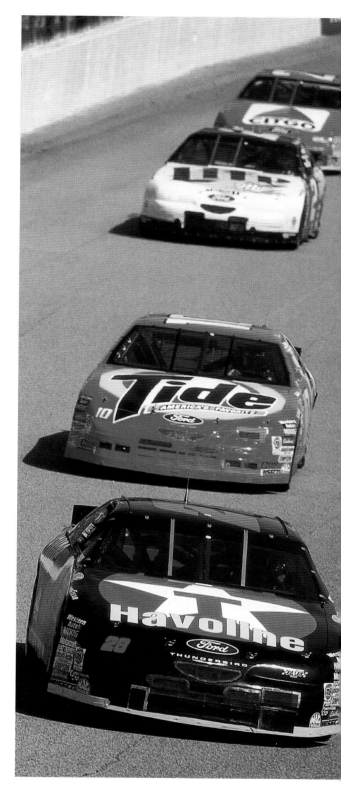

Irvan leads Ricky Rudd at Rockingham, North Carolina, in the early stages of the event on February 23, 1997.

Ernie Irvan just after qualifying well at Bristol Motor Speedway. It was the weekend of his first Winston Cup victory.

# ROBERT VANCE ISAAC 1932-1977

Robert Vance "Bobby" Isaac came into the world knowing firsthand the meaning of the word "heartbreak." Before he was old enough to drive, he had already experienced enough hurt to last a life time. It was the basis for his shy, very quiet and defensive demeanor and the source of his intense drive to make a name for himself in stock car racing. For Isaac, there was no other avenue to travel.

By the time Isaac reached his 13th birthday, his parents, Jerry and Kathy Isaac, had died. With his parents gone, young Bobby was left in the care of his eight brothers and sisters. They could not make him go to school, so he hardly had an education at all. Each of the children was on his own. No one was going to tell them what to do.

Isaac grew up in the country near the Catawba river about 40 miles from Charlotte, North Carolina. The family made their living by growing cotton and corn on the 12 acres of land their father had left to them. It was a hard existence, especially during the winter months.

Isaac found work in an ice plant delivering blocks of ice to customers. Two years passed before he found work in a sawmill. Proceeds from stacking lumber financed his first pair of shoes at 16 years of age. From there, work came in a pool hall and a cotton mill. While drifting from job to job, he happened upon the small dirt track at Hickory, North Carolina, and was immediately hooked on stock car racing. He wanted desperately to drive, and somehow talked his way into the driver's seat of a hobby stock one Saturday night. He lasted only two laps before flipping the car. He was unhurt, but his career had lasted every bit of about two minutes.

There was no doubt racing cars would generate a good living compared to what he had experienced all his life. At the time, he was making 75 cents per hour and barely had enough money in his pocket for a something to eat. All he could do was dream and wait for another opportunity to get behind the wheel.

Then came the break he had longed for.

In 1955, just before his 23rd birthday, Frank Hefner asked Isaac to drive his 1934 Ford Coupe in the Sportsman division. He could drive in return for working on them. His only pay would come from whatever he was able to make on the race track. The arrangement was money in the bank for a driver with Isaac's talent.

Isaac took the car to Columbia, South Carolina, on Thursday; Cowpens, South Carolina,

on Friday; Gaffney, South Carolina, on Saturday; and Harris, North Carolina, on Sunday. Isaac would get a third of his winnings, which translated to about $125 per week—three times what he could make at the saw mill.

Isaac stayed with Hefner through 1957 and worked on his brother-in-law's farm drilling wells in the winter. It was also a time for him to cool off, as several times his hot temper had gotten him in trouble with Pat Purcell, the late executive manager of NASCAR. He was often called down for rough driving and for fighting. Usually, if Isaac got into trouble at the track, Purcell would fine him twice the amount of money he would win from the purse. Isaac was going into the hole fast.

---

> Usually, if Isaac got into trouble at the track, Purcell would fine him twice the amount of money he would win from the purse. Isaac was going into the hole fast.

---

More than once, Isaac was suspended from the Saturday night event but reinstated by the Tuesday race of the following week. It went on between Isaac and Purcell for several years. Some historians claim Isaac was the most fined driver in NASCAR history. Finally, after threats of barring him from NASCAR altogether, Isaac began to control his temper.

Isaac aligned himself with the late Ralph Earnhardt during the 1958 Sportsman season and learned much from the 1956 champion from Kannapolis, North Carolina. Hanging around Earnhardt helped him get into some fashionable racing circles. The result was some relief driving in early Winston Cup (then Grand National) events, first for Jimmy Thompson and later Junior Johnson. Isaac was starting to do well in the small bullrings against the likes of David Pearson and Ned Jarrett, both future champions.

Isaac continued on the local scene until 1962. That year, his dream of driving a Winston Cup car came to fruition with car owner Bondy Long, the one-time supposed heir to the du Pont fortune. Long and Isaac entered 26 events, but crashes and mechanical failures took him out of 14 of them. He left Long's team, citing he couldn't get along with chief mechanic Mack Howard. Later that year, Isaac

drove one race for Smokey Yunick, but crashed after suffering a blown tire.

The break he needed came from Ray Nichels in 1963. It was his first good ride and produced a victory in the 100-mile qualifier at Daytona prior to the 500. Isaac's next win didn't come until five years later.

He did score three second-place finishes, two of those in superspeedway events.

When the Chrysler Hemi engine was banned in 1965, Isaac entered USAC events and won two, again in the Nichels' owned Dodges.

Isaac began driving for Junior Johnson in late 1966 but began to suffer some bad luck, bad finishes, blown engines, and wrecks. He was fired near season's end and thought his career was finished.

In 1967, Isaac joined Nord Krauskopf and crew chief Harry Hyde. It was the beginning of his glory years. They won 3 races in 1968 and 17 of 50 starts in 1969, including his first superspeedway win in December at Texas World Speedway after 56 starts on the big ovals.

Isaac, Kraskpof, and Hyde hit the pinnacle in 1970, winning 11 of 47 starts and the NASCAR championship. Also, on November 24, 1970, Isaac broke the closed course record with a lap of 201.104 mph and was named Driver of the Year by the National Motorsports Association.

In September of 1971, Isaac set 28 stock car records on the Bonneville (Utah) Salt Flats. Most notable was his clocking of 217.368 mph for one kilometer and 216.946 for one mile.

Isaac left the Krauskopf team in September of 1972 after an accident in the Southern 500 at Darlington. With the team he had collected 37 wins and 48 pole positions in 207 starts. The battle Krauskopf had waged with NASCAR over rules and a proposed full schedule with two cars in 1973 fueled Isaac's decision to switch.

Isaac signed with Bud Moore in 1973. Surprisingly, while leading the Talladega 500 on August 12, he elected to retire from racing and brought the car into the pits. His career never again was the same.

There were some good runs with Banjo Matthews in 1974, six races in 1975 and two races in 1976. His last Winston Cup start came on May 30, 1976, when he finished 38th at Charlotte.

On August 13, 1977, Isaac suffered heat exhaustion while driving in a Late Model Sportsman event at Hickory (North Carolina) Speedway. As he exited the car with 25 laps remaining, he fell over the hood of a nearby truck after suffering a heart attack. He died after being admitted to the hospital.

Facing a bright sun, Bobby Isaac anticipates his attempt to break the land speed record in 1971 at the Bonneville Salt Flats in Utah.

In September 1971, Isaac took the number 71 Dodge to the Bonneville Salt Flats. The car ran 216.945 miles per hour.

Isaac driving Junior Johnson's number 26 Ford in the Hickory 250 held April 3, 1966, at Hickory, North Carolina. Johnson is clearing the passenger-side windshield, with Francis Allen cleaning the grille, and Banjo Matthews working on the driver-side glass. Isaac started the event in fifth and finished third.

With the hood up and the engine silent, crew chief Harry Hyde (left) talks with his driver.

Isaac turns hard through the turn during one of his many short tracks races. His stone face shows his intense concentration.

# DALE JARRETT 1956-

One of Dale Jarrett's earliest recollections of Darlington Raceway came in the late summer of 1965. The South Carolina heat and humidity was stifling, enough to make those in the grandstands long for cool relief, just as they had done since the first time automobiles took the green flag at the famed facility in 1950.

Jarrett and several of his friends, mostly the sons of drivers competing on the treacherous one-groove superspeedway, discovered an old football in one of the family station wagons. Soon, a touch game was underway. Their clothes were sweat-soaked and their mothers had already asked them to come sit down and have a cool drink. Just one more touchdown, they would say.

A spirited battle was going on around them, as sheet metal found sheet metal and tire marks scuffed shiny new paint. Father Ned was in tight quarters with Buck Baker, Junior Johnson, Fred Lorenzen, and Darel Dierenger, to name a few. Jarrett's car was having problems with overheating and he was having to turn off his engine on the straightaway each lap.

From time to time, Dale would look up and catch a glimpse of the medium blue No. 11 Ford his father was driving. As if satisfied with his father's progress, Jarrett would go back to the game and make a pass for yardage. A couple more touchdowns were scored on a field marked by cars positioned on the light colored sand in the infield before Jarrett was summoned to go with his mother to watch the final laps. Jarrett's father finally nursed the red-hot engine of his Ford to victory in the Southern 500 by 14 laps over Buck Baker.

Feet planted on Darlington's sacred ground, young Dale stood with mother Martha, sister Patti, and older brother Glen to pose for the cameras. Growing up amidst stock car racing, Dale's career path seemed clear.

Dale Jarrett found victory lane again at Darlington, 32 years after his first visit. On April 23 of 1997, he stood beside his Robert Yates Ford, having won his 10th career NASCAR Winston Cup race. Before the camera once more, the celebration was in his honor as he claimed the last victory at the historic 1.366-mile facility before the track layout was changed.

At the time of his landmark win at Darlington, Jarrett was just as much the racing star his

father was. Short track victories around his North Carolina home slowly propelled him into a one-race ride with former driver and team owner Emmanuel Zervackis at Martinsville, Virginia in 1984. He started 24th, finished 14th and collected $1,515 for his first Winston Cup start. His dream to follow in his famous father's footsteps on NASCAR's highest plateau had finally become reality.

Former team owners Jimmy Means, Mike Curb, Eric Freelander, Ralph Ball, Hoss Ellington, and Buddy Arrington called on Jarrett to wheel their cars before Cale Yarborough included him in his retirement plans of 1989, having him split the schedule with the three-time Winston Cup champion.

At the conclusion of that season, Jarrett found himself without a ride, as Yarborough hired a driver who could bring much needed sponsorship with him to the team. Unknown to him at the time, it was a blessing in disguise.

Neil Bonnett, driver of the Wood Brothers Ford, crashed at Darlington in 1990 and suffered several injuries. Jarrett was tapped to fill the void, thinking the ride was his for a race or two. Bonnett's injuries required a lengthy recovery period, putting Jarrett in the driver's seat for the duration of the season.

In August of 1991, Jarrett went head to head with Davey Allison at Michigan International Speedway and beat the late Alabama driver to the finish line by a foot for his first career Winston Cup win.

The next year, Jarrett received criticism for leaving the Wood Brothers to join the untested Joe Gibbs' organization. Gibbs had found success with the Washington Redskins National Football League team, but came into the racing world at ground zero.

Jarrett brought the team to prominence with a popular victory in the 1993 Daytona 500 over Dale Earnhardt. If anyone had doubts about Jarrett's ability to run at the front, they were quickly erased with the drop of the checkered flag at Daytona International Speedway.

When Robert Yates' driver Ernie Irvan was gravely injured after a serious accident during a practice session at Michigan International Speedway in August of 1994, Jarrett was tapped to drive in relief for the California native, beginning with the 1995 Winston Cup season. Gibbs signed Bobby Labonte, releasing Jarrett from his

contract and freeing him to sign on with Yates.

Jarrett found himself in a no-win position, as the critics didn't feel he was experienced enough to take on such a potent ride. Even though he had driven for other promising teams, some said the team would do nothing but ride for the season.

Jarrett won at Pocono, Pennsylvania, by mid-season and logged several impressive showings. When Irvan miraculously returned for the full season in 1996, Jarrett moved to a second Yates Ford team with crew chief Todd Parrott leading the team. The results were nothing short of dominant.

In 1996, Jarrett won the Daytona 500, the Coca-Cola 600 at Charlotte, North Carolina, the Brickyard 400 at Indianapolis, Indiana, and the Miller 400 at Brooklyn, Michigan. After a season-long bid for the Winston Cup championship, Jarrett finished a close third behind Terry Labonte and Jeff Gordon.

For 1997, Jarrett is once again atop the Winston Cup point standings and is a threat for victory each week. He is proving his critics wrong each time he straps himself into his Yates Ford.

"I don't think anybody knows going into a season how good or bad it's going to be," Jarrett once said. "I think everyone has high expectations whenever you start out and realize you've assembled a good group of individuals to work with and you have the best equipment anyone can have. You expect to do well.

"To think you're going out and win four big races and finish second five times by the time we entered and won Michigan, I don't know if we would have been bold enough to think that's what would happen. Again, you surround yourself with good people and good things are going to happen."

Jarrett poses behind the Oldsmobile owned by Cale Yarborough. The deal was a shared seat with Yarborough. It was Jarrett's first good ride in Winston Cup competition.

Dale Jarrett's first full-time ride was with the Wood Brothers in 1991.

# NED JARRETT 1932-

Throughout his driving career, Ned Jarrett was known as "Gentleman Ned" to his many thousands of fans. His easy-going nature off the track contrasted with his racing demeanor. Jarrett was known as a gambler, often taking chances financially to keep his racing efforts going. Once the green flag dropped, he drove aggressively and knew how to hold his ground. After all, like many racers, the highest finishing position meant the difference between survival and failure. The bills had to be paid.

His easy manner prevailed, even under the worst of circumstances. He rarely raised his voice, even when a fellow driver pinched him into the wall and ended his day.

His easy-going style developed during his childhood, mostly through teachings from his parents, Homer Keith and Eoline Jarrett. Each made sure they sat right alongside their six children at church every Sunday. Church not only taught Jarrett about religion, but it also taught him about driving as he drove the family vehicle, a chopped school bus converted into a truck, to church from the time he was nine years old.

H. K., as Jarrett's father was known, was also an easy-going gentleman, someone highly respected in the small Newton, North Carolina, community. Eoline supported church activities with sweet potato and pecan pies and was there when Sunday dinners were open to the congregation. They were great examples of what parents should be to their children.

Ten miles southwest of Newton was the Jarrett farm, 300 acres H. K. bought from his brothers and sisters upon the death of their father, Oliver J. Jarrett. On that farm, sweet potatoes, cotton, and corn were grown, along with a few head of cattle, hogs, horses, and mules that were raised and sold. The primary family business was the sawmill, a small operation also located on the farm.

In 1943, Jarrett found out how to conduct business. At only 11 years of age he was given an acre of land by his father. It was Jarrett's choice as to what could be grown on it. He chose sweet potatoes, as they paid more per bushel than cotton or corn—that is, if they were planted early enough and avoided a frost. Early potatoes brought $3.25 per bushel, while cotton and corn paid $1.25 per bushel. Over time, Jarrett enjoyed some good payoffs, and at 14 years of age, he accumulated enough profit to buy his first car, a 1941 Ford.

In April 1952, Jarrett first got involved in stock car racing. Out of a friendly poker game,

At Ned Jarrett's last race, an October 30, 1966, outing at Rockingham, he accidentally triggered the fire extinguisher in the cockpit. Despite the resulting unscheduled pit stop, he finished third.

held when a hard rain halted work and shut down the sawmill, Jarrett became half-owner and driver of a car that ran at Hickory (North Carolina) Speedway. He finished 10th in a Limited Sportsman event while driving his 1939 Ford Coupe against the likes of Junior Johnson, Speedy Thompson, and Gywn Staley.

Jarrett's parents placed those who raced cars in one of two categories: bootleggers or a bunch of fools. Since Jarrett never dealt in moonshine, they put him in the second category, but he worked out a compromise with his father. He would be a car owner and continue his office work at the sawmill.

When Jarrett's driver, John Lentz, became ill at the track one night, Jarrett drove using Lentz's name and finished second. The next week he won the race and word traveled quickly back to his father. Finally, Jarrett got his father's blessings, provided he use his own name.

It didn't take long for success to come. Jarrett continued to race at Hickory in 1953 and 1954, all the while winning regularly in the Sportsman division. By September 1955, Jarrett ran his first Winston Cup (then Grand National) event, the Southern 500 at Darlington, South Carolina. Using a new Pontiac provided by Mellie Bernard, he progressed to eighth before something broke on the car. In 1956, he entered Sportsman races around the Southeastern United States. Jarrett won the Sportsman championship in 1957 and 1958.

Jarrett has always been known as a gambler. There was no better example of that than in the summer of 1959. To buy a 1957 Ford Grand National car, Jarrett wrote the required $2,000 check after the bank closed. To cover the check, he had to win races at Myrtle Beach, South Carolina, and the Charlotte (North Carolina) Fairgrounds. With the help of the Lord above and some relief driving from Junior Johnson, due to bloodied hands from severe blisters, Jarrett won both events, his first two victories in what is known to day as Winston Cup racing.

Jarrett went on to win 48 more Winston Cup events in 351 starts with winnings totaling $289,146. Of those wins, his biggest came in

At Hickory (North Carolina) Speedway on April 3, 1966, where Jarrett finished fourth after starting third. It was his final season of competition.

the 1965 Southern 500, where he took the checkered flag 14 laps (or 19.25 miles) ahead of Buck Baker—which is still a record-winning margin. Jarrett the gambler continually turned his engine on and off during the final 20 laps because of overheating problems.

Jarrett won the Winston Cup championship in 1961 and 1965. Both Jarrett and Johnson retired from driving on October 30, 1966, each tied with 50 victories. Had Jarrett known that statistic at the time, he would have tried for 55 wins to overtake Lee Petty, who had 54.

Jarrett was named to the National Motorsports Press Association Hall of Fame in 1972 and went on to become one of stock car racing's leading radio and television broadcasters.

In every venture Jarrett entered, his personal rule was to quit while on top. Jarrett is still the only stock car driver to retire as the reigning champion.

"I have to say I went through good times and a few bad times during my driving career," Jarrett says. "It was tough to make a living driving race cars back then. Still, I'm very grateful to have been a part of it all.

"Driving race cars was very special to me. I always vowed to retire from driving when I was on top and not go down the other side. I retired as reigning champion in 1966. At the time, we compared ourselves with athletes of others professions. Most people thought reaction time for a driver wavered about the time they hit their thirties. Since those days, its been proven through Richard Petty, Harry Gant, Dick Trickle and a few others that drivers can be successful in their 50s. Had I known then what I know now, I wouldn't have retired as early as I did. Race drivers can go longer and be quite effective. There have been times I wished I would have driven longer and not retired when I did. But then again, my family is very important to me and by retiring when I did, I was able to watch my children grow up. Being able to do that is very special to me."

# JUNIOR JOHNSON 1931-

**R**obert Glen "Junior" Johnson, the 5-foot 11-inch 240-pound chicken farmer from the mountains of Wilkes County, North Carolina, carved a successful motorsports career with little more than a few bucks and some common sense. His willingness to work hard and accept nothing but the best in himself and others made him an American legend. It was a way of thinking that saved his life and brought to him a life of wealth and recognition through nearly 40 years of racing.

Johnson came to stock car racing after building his own driving talent on the winding mountain roads near his Ingle Hollow, North Carolina, home. He tackled those hairpin turns not for the thrill of mastering them, but rather to escape the law enforcement officials on his tail. Along with his father, Robert Glen, and brothers, L. P. and Fred, Johnson began hauling moonshine at the age of 15. Johnson once said, "To us brothers, it was just like a milk run. It was just business—plain and simple."

The chases went on as many as five times per week, but the Johnson boys never got caught on the highway. The net did fall down upon them, however, on June 2, 1956.

Johnson and his father were caught making white liquor at the family still and charged with dealing nontax paid whiskey. Junior pleaded guilty to the charge on November 27, 1956, and received a two-year prison sentence and a $5,000 fine. He was paroled after serving 11 months and 3 days. On December 27, 1957, he walked out of prison a free man. He was eventually pardoned by former President Ronald Reagan in the late 1980s.

Johnson won his first NASCAR race on May 7, 1955, at Hickory, North Carolina, but his life's dream was to become a major league baseball pitcher. When he was 16, a tractor accident hurt his pitching arm and eliminated any hope of a baseball career. Immediately after being released from prison, he elected to go back into stock car racing to help support his family. The money wasn't bad as far as winners' purses were concerned, and racing in cow pastures wasn't illegal, unless one did so without the land owner's permission.

As a driver, Johnson won 50 NASCAR Winston Cup (then Grand National) races (including the 1960 Daytona 500) and 46 pole posi-

tions in 309 starts between 1951 and 1966. He earned $276,045 with his best season coming in 1965 with 13 wins that year, 10 pole positions, and $57,825 in season earnings.

In the early 1960s, fellow driver Fred Lorenzen broke into what was to be a conversation with Johnson about investing money. It was a short conversation, as the soft-spoken Johnson routinely said little and talked through his actions on the race track.

"I've been buying stock in Esso [now Exxon] and a few other big companies with most of my race winnings. Where are you putting your money, Junior?"

Johnson, a man limited on education and worldly exposure, answered Lorenzen by say-

---

"I've been buying stock in Esso . . . with my race winnings. Where are you putting your money, Junior?"
—*Fred Lorenzen*

"I puts my money in my jeans!"
—*Junior's response*

---

ing, "I puts my money in my jeans!"

On October 30, 1966, at Rockingham, North Carolina, Johnson ran his last race as a driver. For the remainder of the 1966 season until the Daytona 500 of 1971, Johnson campaigned Ford products. When the auto maker elected to stage one of its many withdrawals from racing, Johnson threatened to quit racing, once and for all. But some strong encouragement from Richard Howard, his longtime friend and former head of Charlotte Motor Speedway, prompted Johnson to bring Chevrolet back into the NASCAR arena in a time when factory support from the auto maker was dead because of rules conflicts. Ironically, it was Johnson who gave Chevrolet its last wins, eight total that year, without any of the company's money.

Johnson re-emerged with a 1971 Chevrolet Monte Carlo in October of that year with Char-

lie Glotzbach at the wheel. Success was limited, but the next year, Johnson teamed with Bobby Allison and won an impressive 10 victories and 11 pole positions.

The glorious season got Johnson a lot of attention. Writer Thomas Wolfe penned an article for *Esquire* magazine that prompted Hollywood to make a movie loosely based on Johnson's life called, *The Last American Hero.*

By late 1972, Allison and Johnson were at odds over most everything with communication between the two almost nonexistent. When Howard had a chance to sign Cale Yarborough, he called Allison in the early morning hours while in Riverside, California, for a Trans Am race, and said, "Bobby, we need to know if you're coming back in 1973. We have the chance right now to get the best driver in NASCAR." Allison, half-asleep and agitated by the bluntness of the call, responded, "Get him," and slammed down the phone. Had Allison been awake, the course of history would have taken an entirely different turn.

From there, Johnson began to build his brilliant legacy. From 1973 through 1980 his team racked up 55 victories, 50 pole positions, and 3 NASCAR Winston Cup championships in 1976, 1977, and 1978, respectively, with driver Cale Yarborough.

With Darrell Waltrip, the Johnson team won 3 more Winston Cup titles, 43 victories, as well as 34 pole positions from 1981 through 1985. The late Neil Bonnett, Terry Labonte, Geoff Bodine, Sterling Marlin, Hut Stricklin, and Bill Elliott added 16 more victories and 24 more pole positions. With 192 victories and nearly $20 million in earnings to his credit, counting his days as a driver, Johnson left his mark on the sport when he retired from racing at the end of the 1995 Winston Cup season. His departure marked the end of NASCAR's most colorful era.

Johnson is known as one of the smartest drivers and mechanics to turn a steering wheel or wrench in the history of stock car racing. A brilliant innovator, he was blessed with a backwoods sensibility that his fans could relate to. It's ironic that such wealth came to a man who never finished high school.

Simply put, he was one of stock car racing's most successful pioneers, both in his own career and in those of the sport's biggest names.

Another hot day at Darlington on September 4, 1972. Bobby Allison won the race in a Junior Johnson-prepared Chevrolet.

Johnson driving in the 1962 Darlington 500.

Johnson and Cotton Owens.

Johnson with Linda Vaughn in 1963 at the National 500 in Charlotte, North Carolina. Linda Vaughn was "Miss Firebird" for Pure Oil Company.

Johnson with *National Speed Sport News* editor Chris Economaki at the 1962 Darlington 500.

Bobby Allison wins the Southern 500 at Darlington, South Carolina, held on September 4, 1972. From left to right is crew member Herb Nab, Allison, car builder Johnson, and victory lane coordinator Bill Brodrick.

Johnson passes a gas can back over the wall during a pit stop in the 1973 Southern 500 held at Darlington Raceway. Cale Yarborough drove the Johnson-prepared number 11 car to victory that day.

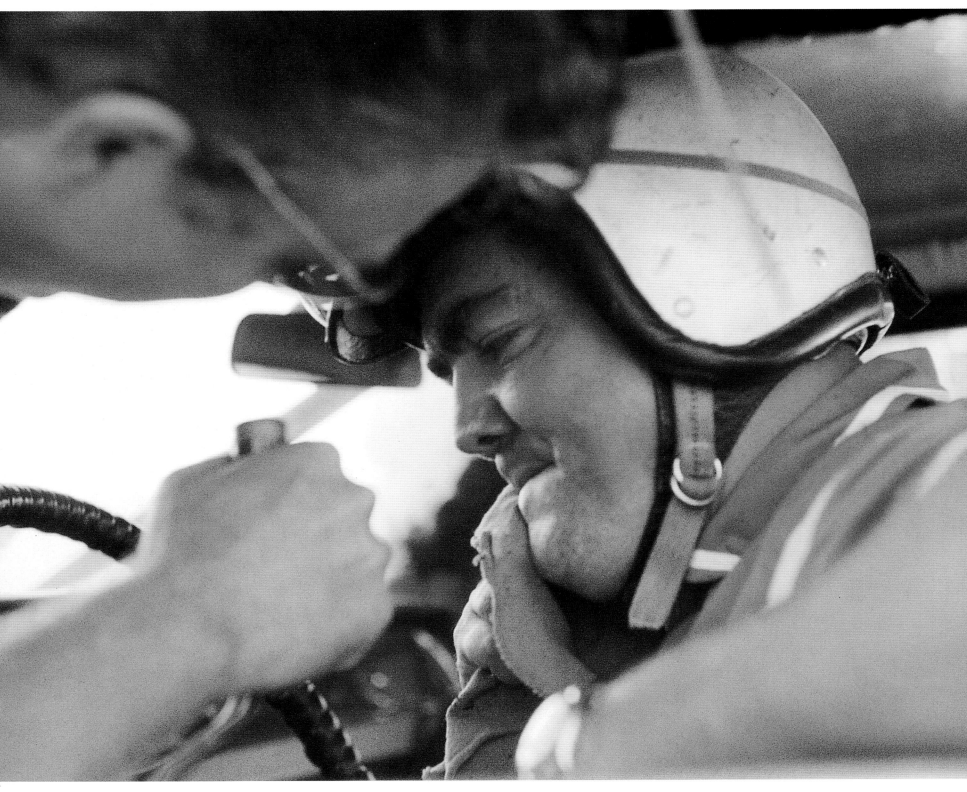

Johnson at Charlotte Motor Speedway. "Big" Bill Ward is doing the radio interview.

# ALAN KULWICKI 1954-1993

Few people who worked for Alan Kulwicki would say their relationship was pleasant. His obsession with perfection often created ill feelings and disgusted crewmen. He was intense and difficult, often short to those around him. Such behavior is typical of a perfectionist, and Kulwicki was, without a doubt, a staunch perfectionist.

One couldn't really blame Kulwicki for his style of management. They were his cars running off of his budget, one that was often very light in balance. Still, the Wisconsin native would consistently make his presence known among the top contenders for the win. His mechanical mind ran with the precision of a quartz clock. The wheels were always turning, 24 hours a day, always searching for a way to make his Fords run faster and more efficiently.

Kulwicki discovered stock car racing as a teenager and attacked it like a hungry animal. His father, a builder of racing engines on the USAC circuit, had tried to subtly discourage his son, having seen the trails and tribulations firsthand. Still, Gerald Kulwicki's son had a definite love for cars and an inner fire that wouldn't extinguish quickly.

In 1974, Kulwicki started his first stock car race at Haley's Corners (Wisconsin) Speedway at 19 years of age. Later that summer, he won a feature event at Leo's Speedway in Oshkosh, Wisconsin. There was no doubt he had found himself through racing. He was innovative and reasoned he could produce winning cars with his two hands. His choice to study engineering in college proved to be a blessing over the next three years of racing.

Kulwicki was an inventor. Having the inability to see the right rear corner of his race car in the standard rearview mirror prompted him to develop a multiangle mirror, as well as a baffled exhaust system for race cars. He also invented a wheel balancing system used in Indy car racing.

In 1979, Kulwicki won the track championship at Slinger and KauKauna, prompting him to make the decision to race full time. Running races in the USAC stock car division as well as the ASA (American Speed Association) helped promote him as a winner with 5 victories and 12 pole positions. It was time to advance further into his plan.

By 1984, Kulwicki ran five NASCAR Busch Series races and All Pro races. The next year, Bill Terry, a Greenville, South Carolina, busi-

nessman, offered Kulwicki five events in the NASCAR Winston Cup circuit. Later that year, Kulwicki sold his equipment and decided a move to the South would be beneficial. Winston Cup was where he wanted to be.

In the winter months of 1985, Kulwicki was set for the trip to North Carolina when his truck burned due to an electrical fire. Eventually, he found another vehicle to pull his trailer and equipment and arrived in Concord, a town just north of Charlotte, North Carolina. He rented shop space from longtime Winston Cup mechanic and car builder Norman Negre and entered 23 Winston Cup races in 1986. With only one car and two engines, he won Rookie of the Year and completed 94.7 percent of possible laps in the process. His first top-five finish came April 27 of that year at Martinsville, Virginia.

In 1987, Kulwicki bought the equipment from Terry and changed his number from 35 to 7. On March 8, he won his first pole position at Richmond, Virginia. He moved to a new shop in an industrial park in Concord and obtained used office furniture that had been discarded from another race team after their redecorating project.

On November 8, 1988, Kulwicki finally found victory lane at Phoenix, Arizona. His was the first display of what he called a "Polish Victory Lap," a clockwise lap around the speedway. He won four pole positions that year and six more the next. Kulwicki had arrived on the Winston Cup circuit and was successful with the leanest of resources.

By 1990, Kulwicki moved again to a custom-built facility near Charlotte Motor Speedway. Another win came at Rockingham, North Carolina, and so did a healthy dose of respect from the highly financed teams. Kulwicki's name made its rounds in some of the sport's biggest rides. Topping the list was Junior Johnson, who wanted the new star to wheel his Fords. Kulwicki considered the offer and turned him and the lucrative financial package down. Within the Winston Cup circuit, Kulwicki's critics were out in force, sure he had hit his head on one too many walls. Kulwicki, however, had a long-range plan, and Johnson wasn't part of it.

Reportedly, the primary sponsor he had lined up for 1991 went to Johnson in the 12th hour, leaving Kulwicki with hardly any financing just weeks before the season opening Daytona 500. With a one-race deal from the U.S. Army, the team did enter the race, but the immediate future looked bleak. The next three races were funded from Kulwicki's personal bank account.

With a pole position at Atlanta Motor

Speedway in March of that year, a major sponsor found its way onto the quarter panels of his refrigerator-white Ford. A win at Bristol, Tennessee, prompted that sponsor to sign him for a three-year deal.

Then came 1992, a year that will always be remembered as a true David and Goliath battle for the championship between Kulwicki and the big dollar teams. That year, Kulwicki was the definition of consistency where finishes were concerned. He was victorious twice, at Pocono, Pennsylvania, and again at Bristol. Also, there were 11 top-5 finishes, 17 top 10s, and 6 pole positions, more than any other driver that year.

He went into the final race of the season at Atlanta Motor Speedway on November 15 as one of six drivers battling for the elusive 1992 title. By the halfway point, attrition and accidents left only two of the title contenders on the track, Kulwicki and Bill Elliott in Johnson's Ford. Kulwicki's crew calculated that by leading the most laps, and thereby gaining a 10-point bonus, he could win the championship regardless of what Elliott did. As it turned out, Kulwicki led 103 laps and finished second. Elliott led for 102 laps and won the race, but not the title.

The 1992 Winston Cup Championship was the crown jewel of Kulwicki's career, won by a mere 10 points (4,078 to 4,068), the closest margin in NASCAR's modern era. He was the first driver to come from behind to take the title since Richard Petty overtook Darrell Waltrip in the last race of the 1979 season, and he was the first champion to hold a college degree.

In the first four events of 1993, Kulwicki was 26th at Daytona; 4th at Rockingham, 3rd at Richmond, 36th after a crash at Atlanta, Georgia, and 6th at Darlington, South Carolina.

On April 1, 1993, Kulwicki made an appearance and was en route to Bristol, when the Merlin Fairchild twin engine airplane in which he was a passenger crashed after taking a nose-dive a few miles shy of the Tri-Cities Regional Airport near Blountville, Tennessee. Also on board the plane were Mark Brooks, 26; Dan Duncan, 44; and pilot Charlie Campbell, 48. All four people died in the fiery crash.

Just four months earlier, on December 4, 1992, Kulwicki concluded his Winston Cup championship acceptance speech by saying, "I hope that when 1993 is over the people at Winston, the people at NASCAR, and the competitors all look back and say, 'We were proud to have him represent us as our champion.'"

*Alan Kulwicki early in his rookie season, 1986. Note that his name is misspelled on his Ford.*

# TERRY LABONTE 1956-

From his quiet mannerisms and equally soft spoken voice, one would think two-time Winston Cup champion Terry Labonte would be more comfortable with a golf club in his hands rather than behind the wheel of a 700-horsepower race car. Labonte chose the latter at a very early age with the support of his father, Bob Labonte.

The progression was quite the usual, starting with quarter midgets in 1964 and a later graduation to dirt short tracks around his native Corpus Christi, Texas, home. Labonte followed the Winston Cup circuit by way of radio whenever stations in the area would carry races. While listening to Richard Petty, Cale Yarborough, Bobby Allison, David Pearson, and other racing legends battle door handle to door handle on the superspeedways, Labonte nursed a deep inner desire to take part in those skirmishes. There was no doubt in his mind he was good enough to make a living from Winston Cup racing. There was only one way to accomplish his lifelong dream; move to North Carolina, the heart of stock car racing.

Labonte had one ace in his pocket. Texas oil man Billy Hagan sponsored Labonte in races around the state of Texas. Hagan, a racer in his own right, couldn't resist the temptation to build a Winston Cup team from the ground up. Early into the 1975 season, Hagan's operation was up and running. Labonte joined Hagan's operation two years later. Surprisingly, though, not as the driver. That chore belonged to Skip Manning, another Hagan protégé who won Rookie of the Year honors in 1976. Labonte had to settle for a job as a crew member.

To say Labonte missed Texas and his family was an understatement. There was little money, no ride for him on the local North Carolina short track scene, and plenty of reasons to want to return home. Through phone calls between father and son, Bob Labonte convinced his son to stay, as the possibility of a break could come his way.

Relations between Manning and Hagan began to deteriorate by late summer of 1978 and finally ended on August 6 of that year after

Manning's 38th-place finish at Talladega, Alabama. Hagan turned to Mel Larson to drive at Brooklyn, Michigan, and sat out at Bristol, Tennessee.

Labonte saw the opening he longed for. After several discussions, Hagan relented and gave Labonte the ride. Labonte proved his worth immediately by finishing fourth in the grueling Southern 500 at Darlington, South Carolina, behind Cale Yarborough, Richard Petty, and Darrell Waltrip. His dreams of driving competitively against NASCAR's best had finally come true.

Hagan had found his star, but wasn't totally convinced he could handle the car week to week. Labonte drove in relief for Dick May at Dover, Delaware, the next week and brought the car home 10th. Seat time was what Labonte needed most, but he continued to share races with May, as not to lose rookie status for the following season.

---

> Labonte nursed a deep inner desire to take part in those skirmishes. There was no doubt in his mind he was good enough to make a living from Winston Cup racing.

---

Labonte and Hagan ditched the No. 92 for No. 44 at the start of the 1979 season, marking a new beginning to their long-term partnership. The finishes were consistent and equipment was holding together. Labonte finished third at Darlington, South Carolina, setting the stage for a stellar career. Labonte made 31 starts that year, with two top-five finishes and 13 top tens, netting him a 10th-place finish in the Winston Cup point standings. Dale Earnhardt bested Labonte, Harry Gant, and Joe Millikan for Rookie of the Year honors.

Labonte's love affair with Darlington gave him his first win in the 1980 Southern 500 and still ranks as one of the biggest upsets in the race's

history. Leaders David Pearson and Dale Earnhardt hit an oil slick in turn one, caused by Frank Warren's blown engine. Labonte trailed two seconds behind and won the race under caution. It established him as an up and coming contender.

The consistency continued and in 1984, Labonte gave Hagan his only Winston Cup championship to date. From the outside, it looked as though relations between the champion and the team owner were at an all-time high, but in the shadows, problems loomed. By 1987, Labonte moved over to Junior Johnson's organization, then known as one of the top teams of the tour. Limited success came with Johnson through 1989, as was the case with team owners Richard Jackson in 1990, and a surprise reunion with Hagan in 1991. The union lasted through 1993, and since his championship nearly 10 years earlier, there were only six victories to Labonte's credit and none with Jackson or the reunion with Hagan.

The critics came out in force , saying that Labonte was on the downhill slide, that the glory has passed him by.

Then another surprise occurred.

Ricky Rudd elected to leave Hendrick Motorsports to start his own Winston Cup organization. Labonte's name surfaced as a possible replacement and, after his strong finish at North Wilkesboro, North Carolina, in late 1993, team owner Rick Hendrick was convinced he had found his man.

The union has produced more victories than with any other team owner in his career (eight) and a rebirth as a contender with his 1996 NASCAR Winston Cup championship.

Labonte usually shows no emotion. Whether enjoying the festivities of victory lane or checking damage to his race car after a spin, one never knows what he's thinking. When he emerged from his Hendrick Motorsports Chevrolet in November of 1996, there was definite emotion on his face and in his voice.

"That's the first time I've ever gotten emotional," Labonte says of his special day. "I couldn't believe it. I was a little surprised at myself. It was something I've worked for for a long, long time."

Consistent finishes brought Terry Labonte a hard-earned 1996 Winston Cup Championship over fellow Hendrick team driver Jeff Gordon.

Terry Labonte was declared Winston Cup champion after a strong third-place finish at Riverside, California, on November 12, 1984. Here he holds the champion's trophy the morning after the race.

Labonte is not one to display a lot of emotion in public. His race face remains impassive through the most trying times.

Labonte discusses strategy with Junior Johnson during an open practice session at Charlotte Motor Speedway in May 1986.

Labonte makes a pit stop at North Wilkesboro, North Carolina, en route to winning the Holly Farms 400 in a Junior Johnson-owned Chevrolet on October 4, 1987.

# FRED LORENZEN 1934-

After a race, Fred Lorenzen would usually go directly from his race car to a phone booth to call his stockbroker and spend the money he had just won. The once-poor midwesterner came to stock car racing because of what it offered him financially. By the time he was 31 years old, he possessed lavish cars, boats, and more money than he felt he could ever spend. At the advice of his New York stockbroker, he retired on April 2, 1967, after becoming the first driver to win more than $100,000 in a single season. Lorenzen looks back on that decision daily from his Elmhurst, Illinois, home and feels it was the worst mistake he ever made.

"I was stupid to quit," Lorenzen says often today. "I had won everything NASCAR had to offer. The stockbroker told me one day to forget it and enjoy life. But what I enjoyed most was racing, and I just gave it away. I quit too soon."

His fans affectionately nicknamed him "Fearless Freddie" and "The Golden Boy" for his blonde hair, handsomely chiseled looks, and overwhelming charisma. He was a pubic relations dream in an era when NASCAR desperately needed a superstar in the press. Like Mickey Mantle was to baseball and Johnny Unitas was to professional football, Lorenzen was an attractive, likable hero any sports fan could appreciate.

Before the glory, Lorenzen was the typical teenager growing up in Chicago. His first endeavor with automobiles came when he and several of his buddies placed bets as to which one of them would be the first to roll a 1937 Plymouth in a vacant field. Lorenzen held on for the ride and claimed the bragging rights.

Lorenzen supported himself by working in a local service station where he housed a 1952 Oldsmobile, a car he fondly referred to as "the four-wheel bomb." When challenged on a long narrow strip called "Country Line Road," he would discard several hundred pounds of weight by stripping anything that could be tossed out before wasting any of his challengers.

Graduation from the strip meant racing at the Milwaukee (Wisconsin) State Fairgrounds, but Lorenzen had limited success. Just by chance, he became acquainted with Ralph Moody, a hotshoe driver who was winning every week at Milwaukee and making it look easy. That relationship would later pay off in spades.

Lorenzen won the USAC title on two occasions, in 1958 and 1959. In 1956 Lorenzen tried his hand at NASCAR racing, but never had the equipment to showcase this talent. Like many before him, he returned to the midwest-

Fred Lorenzen wins the World 600 on May 23, 1965, at Charlotte, North Carolina, in a Holman-Moody Ford.

> Like Mickey Mantle was to baseball and Johnny Unitas was to professional football, Lorenzen was an attractive, likable hero any sports fan could appreciate.

ern states to rebuild his local short track career and pray for another opportunity in NASCAR.

As fate would have it, Lorenzen had been noticed for what he could do with a race car. On Christmas Eve of 1960, he received a phone call from Moody. Moody had connections with Ford Motor Company and was part of the famed Holman-Moody operation, the stock car production factory for Ford that fielded several cars for several top-name drivers of the era. Despite Lorenzen's belief that he was at a disadvantage to southern drivers, Moody wanted him.

"At first, I thought Moody was joking," Lorenzen says. "I hadn't had a good year in 1960 and I really thought he was playing a joke. But he said he was serious and offered me

Lorenzen sports a knowing look as he hoists his winner's trophy in the air after winning the 1964 Rebel 300 on May 9, 1964.

a ride. Deep inside I knew I could win. His calling me was a dream come true."

The Lorenzen, Holman, and Moody union saw great success. On the race track, Lorenzen battled with the likes of Fireball Roberts, Marvin Panch, Junior Johnson, Ned Jarrett, and Curtis Turner, to name a few. On 26 occasions from 1961 through 1967, Lorenzen beat them and made his mark in the record books.

The success he enjoyed helped to establish himself in the headlines. "Fearless Freddie" had a hold on the sport when severe stomach ulcers began to plague his health.

Then came what was thought to be his retirement around the 1.522-mile track in Atlanta, Georgia, on April 2, 1967. Those in attendance were telling him good-bye, but he would return to the track. Lorenzen made sporadic attempts at coming back from 1970 through 1972, but the glory years were behind him. He turned to a very successful career in real estate sales and worked in race broadcasting on occasion.

Lorenzen and Junior Johnson confer on August 7, 1966, at the Dixie 400 held at Atlanta International Raceway. Lorenzen is driving Johnson's "yellow banana" number 26 Ford.

left: Lorenzen talking with John Holman.

below: Joe Weatherly (8) goes fender to fender with Lorenzen (28) during the National 400 at Charlotte Motor Speedway. Weatherly finished fifth, while Lorenzen bested him by two positions to finish third.

right: During a pit stop at Charlotte Motor Speedway, Lorenzen takes a swallow of a cold drink after some hard-fought laps.

# DEWAYNE "TINY" LUND 1936–1975

Dewayne "Tiny" Lund lived his life as if it would end by sundown. The term "half throttle" was nowhere to be found in his personal dictionary, whether on the track or on the farm. There was simply too much to accomplish and too much fun to be had.

That same live-to-the-limit style brought forth two sides of Lund.

First, there was a pleasant, peaceful side. He cherished hugs from children, enjoyed the beautiful scenery around his fish camp, loved to pet dogs that lay at his feet, smiled at the thought of memorable fishing trips with close friends, and gave generously to the poor. His heart was as big as his towering frame.

His pleasant side included a spirit full of mischief. The practical jokes he played on any unsuspecting soul who came into his trap were legendary. Once while fellow driver Cale Yarborough napped in his hotel room after a long day at the track, Lund stormed through the locked door, grabbed the double bed mattress with his bear-like hands, and carried it down a flight of stairs to the pool. Yarborough, still attached to the mattress and hanging on for dear life, went into the pool with it, kicking and screaming the entire flight. As Yarborough stood stunned and soaked, Lund roared with laughter as tears filled his eyes.

Then, the dark side.

After a hard-fought contest had gone bad, one would not want to be opposite Lund. At 6 feet, 5 inches and built like a tank, he could be bad news to the guy facing him eye to eye. As far as Lund was concerned, fair was fair, but anything less meant a visit at the other driver's side window. The sight of him coming was unnerving.

On the other hand, if Lund occasionally pinched someone off into a guard rail for the win, the opposing driver would be steaming and confront Lund, only to be met with a heavy arm around his shoulders and an understanding smile.

While in high school, Lund turned down numerous scholarships to play football, choosing to race instead. He found his niche at the fairgrounds of Harland, Iowa, at age 16. One summer evening, Lund entered a motorcycle race and his parents were in the grandstands. When the stock cars took to the field afterward, Mr. Lund noticed a car unnervingly similar to

---

At 6 feet, 5 inches and built like a tank, Lund was bad news to the guy facing him eye to eye.

---

the Lund family vehicle circling the turns. His son was aboard, passing everything in sight.

His first NASCAR event came on October 9, 1955, at Lehi, Arkansas. On the 66th lap, he crashed on the 1.5-mile high-banked dirt track and nearly died. He was thrown from his car after a series of flips and was struck by the front wheels of another car as he lay on the track. His recuperation took several months, as he suffered a broken back in the accident.

A year passed before Lund resumed racing. From 1957 through 1962, he drifted from ride to ride, looking for a solid deal. While at Daytona in 1963 as a bystander, he helped to rescue driver Marvin Panch after he suffered severe burns in a fiery sports car accident. For his heroic efforts, Lund was given Panch's ride for the 500 in the Wood Brothers Ford and won

the race over Fred Lorenzen. It was his only major win in NASCAR.

Another victory came in 1965 at Columbia, South Carolina, and another at Bowman Gray Stadium in Winston-Salem, North Carolina, in 1966. Entries in the Grand Touring division (later called Grand American division) produced 37 wins and three championships from 1968 through 1971. Lund seemed too busy enjoying his newfound success to enter events in NASCAR's biggest arena.

Lund entered the 1973 World 600 at Charlotte, but suffered a blown engine. His final Winston Cup event came on August 16, 1975, at Talladega, Alabama. On the seventh lap, Lund's Dodge was T-boned in the driver's side door during a multicar crash. He died eight minutes after the crash from massive internal injuries.

Buddy Baker, one of Lund's closest friends, won the race but was not informed of his death until the postrace interview.

"Tiny was my buddy," Baker says. "The day he died, I was in the press box giving the winner's interview and feeling great about the win. Someone blurted out, 'Oh, by the way, Tiny was killed in the race today.' It was the biggest shock of my life. I got the strength to stand up and I excused myself. I just simply had to leave.

"People still talk about Tiny just like he was here today. He had a heart as big as the state of North Carolina, and he was absolutely the very best there was when he was in good equipment.

"If he ever got mad at you, you were in trouble. To see him coming at you mad was an awesome sight. If he ever hit you, you always hoped you landed on your feet so you could at least get a good start running. You never wanted him to be able to hit you twice."

Tiny Lund uses a pit road water hose to fight the summer heat on May 28, 1967, at Charlotte Motor Speedway.

After a long, hot day of racing on April 3, 1964, Lund takes a breather in the pits.

Humpy Wheeler of the Firestone Tire Company gets a big hand from Lund at Atlanta Motor Speedway in the spring of 1966.

Through the first turn at Hickory on April 3, 1964, Lund hangs on to the steering wheel of his Ford.

# DAVE MARCIS 1941-

Since the day he rolled into NASCAR Winston Cup racing in February 1968, Dave Marcis has sported his reliable wing-tip dress shoes each time he's tossed his leg through the driver's side window of his cars. Marcis never wavered from his conservative style, even during the brief years he enjoyed good rides.

Marcis, a Wisconsin native transplanted to North Carolina, is the last of the hard-core independent drivers, those who've competed in Winston Cup racing without the luxury of handsome sponsorship. Instead, they travel from race to race, skimping on parts, food, and equipment, in hopes of finishing well to help finance their next event. Somewhere in between, they milk out a modest living to pay their bills at home.

With a gold mine of cars at his disposal from his father's wrecking yard, Marcis could pick and choose his early dirt-track equipment. Once hooked to the junkyard wrecker, he would pull his newfound treasure close enough to reach the torch lines to create his next ride. He practiced for races by speeding around the vacant areas of the junkyard.

Short-track success eventually gave reason to head south to NASCAR's domain. With nothing more than a few bucks and a lot of determination, Marcis wrote to NASCAR for a rule book and built a car in the dead of a cold Wisconsin winter. The early years saw him make lengthy trips from the Midwest to the East Coast, but to cut costs, he moved to Avery's Creek, North Carolina by 1971.

While running well against the high-dollar teams of the 1970s, Marcis' name was mentioned in many circles as a good candidate for more lucrative rides. He was finally persuaded to park his own cars and was given the Dodges of Ray Nichels in 1971 and American Motors Matadors of Roger Penske in 1972. It wasn't until 1975 that he became victorious in his 225th start while

Marcis runs hard in his 1971 Dodge at Charlotte on May 30, 1971. He finished ninth.

---

Marcis was often outspoken and opinionated and cared little for team owners who held him back in two-car efforts allowing bigger name drivers to win when his cars were capable of doing so.

---

driving for Nord Krauskopf at Martinsville, Virginia. That same year, he finished second to Richard Petty in the NASCAR Winston Cup point standings.

In 1976, three more wins came. But Marcis was often outspoken and opinionated and cared little for team owners who held him back in two-car efforts allowing bigger name drivers to win when his cars were capable of doing so.

In 1979, he went back to fielding his own cars, and his last win came at Rich-mond, Virginia, in 1982. Aside from 30 races in 1984 with the team of Bob Rahilly and Butch Mock and seven events in 1992 with Larry Hedrick, Marcis has fielded his own teams since.

On July 6, 1996, he completed his 800th career start at Daytona International Speedway. It was a milestone second only to Petty, who started an incredible 1,185 races.

"I enjoy racing," Marcis says. "It's been my life. I enjoy the sport. I started when I was 16 years old monkeying around up in Wisconsin. I raced for 10 years, then came to NASCAR. So I've been racing my entire life.

"When you consider what we have to operate with against the peak teams, I think we've really accomplished something. I think we've had some great success. There's been a lot of ups and a lot of downs, but that's common in any type of work you do."

September 6, 1971, was a hot day of racing at the Darlington Raceway in South Carolina. Dave Marcis started his 1971 Nichels-Goldsmith prepared Plymouth fifth and finished there.

# STERLING MARLIN 1957-

As far back as he can remember, the sounds of race engines roaring and welders crackling filled Sterling Marlin's ears. Racing was a way of life for Marlin, just as it once was for his dad, Clifton "Coo Coo" Marlin. A stock car of some type sat in the shed out back throughout his formative years.

When "Coo Coo" bought his best car, a 1972 Chevrolet Monte Carlo from Junior Johnson, young Sterling was outraged that his parents made him attend school rather than go with a group of guys to North Carolina to pick up the car. He customarily would get off the school bus and walk right into the race shop, often staining his school books with shop grease. His mother, the late Eula Faye Marlin, eventually cut paper sacks into book covers for her son's books.

At 15 years old, Marlin helped on the pit crew during the summer. On occasion, his cousin let the underaged driver take the wheel of the transporter on the long trips from Columbia, Tennessee, to places like Michigan, Daytona, or Texas. When school was in session, Marlin worked on his dad's cars but stayed home to play football for his local high school.

Marlin finally got the chance to fulfill his dream of driving stock cars by age 16. With help from his father's Winston Cup sponsor, H. B. Cunningham, Marlin purchased a 1966 Chevelle to race at the Nashville Speedway. A great deal of success followed, but not until an unexpected venture came his way. In only his third start in a race car, Marlin relieved his father in a Winston Cup event at Nashville on July 17, 1976, and finished eighth.

The following year, Sterling and his father devised a plan to break the news to Mrs. Marlin of Sterling's intentions to drive an ARCA car at Talladega, Alabama. With both cars loaded on trailers behind the shop, the two went into the family home for dinner. For several minutes, all that could be heard was silverware cutting food on china. Finally, Sterling's father broke the ice by saying, "Pass the potatoes. Sterling is going to drive at Talladega." A couple of seconds passed before Mrs. Marlin began expressing her dislike for the idea. Short tracks were fine, but to drive on the superspeedways was out of the question for her only son. With that, the two male Marlins rose

Marlin is strapped in and ready, awaiting the command to fire his engine on March 6, 1988, at Rockingham, North Carolina.

Marlin never let the wins taint his easy-going personality. The fame and fortune he acquired through NASCAR racing simply hasn't changed him.

from the table, stuffing their mouths with food and pockets with cornbread.

Both ran to their respective car haulers and set out for Alabama, leaving Mrs. Marlin behind. They waved good-bye and headed down the long dirt road of the family farm. From that day forward, Marlin competed on the superspeedways, while his mother slowly warmed to the idea. It was not an easy sell.

Marlin continued on the short tracks and won three consecutive track championships at the Nashville Speedway in 1980, 1981, and 1982. Marlin campaigned the full Winston Cup schedule in 1983 and went on to win Rookie of the Year honors while driving for former driver and team owner Roger Hamby. Marlin struggled with various team owners until 1986, when he joined Billy Hagan for four full seasons. Two more seasons with Junior Johnson

and a season with Stavola Brothers Racing set the stage for his greatest success with Morgan-McClure Racing.

After nine second-place finishes, Marlin's first victory came in the 1994 Daytona 500 in February of that year. He defended his Daytona 500 crown the next year and added four more victories, two at Talladega, one at Darlington, and a win at Daytona in July.

Marlin has never let the wins taint his easy-going country personality. The fame and fortune he acquired through NASCAR racing simply hasn't changed him.

"Stock car racing is all I've ever known," Marlin says. "NASCAR has been real good to me and my family.

"To win the Daytona 500 back to back is a real dream come true, but of course, anytime you win in Winston Cup it's really great. I know there are some good things to come in my future, maybe even a Winston Cup championship someday. Still, no matter what happens, I'm always just going to be myself because I really don't think of myself as a celebrity. I'm just Sterling Marlin. Racing is all I've ever done."

Sterling Marlin has lived and breathed stock car racing since childhood when his father's stock cars were a regular fixture on the Marlin family farm.

# MARK MARTIN 1959-

Since the early 1970s, Mark Martin has been associated with stock car racing like salt has been associated to pepper. With a youthful face and short frame to match, Martin looked too young to drive on a busy highway, much less on a high-banked speedway.

Year after year, he quietly established himself as a top contender in the Winston Cup and Busch Series divisions of NASCAR and could refer to himself as "the quiet aggressor."

The early years of his career were no different. If there was a race to win, Martin had the talent and equipment to mix it up with the very best. To the surprise of many, he battled veteran drivers, such as Bobby Allison, Dick Trickle, and Jim Sauter, for American Speed Association (ASA) victories. Long before he was of legal age, he mastered the tracks of the Midwest better than some with twice the experience. Martin racked up hundreds of wins as well as four ASA championships.

Martin didn't move into the Winston Cup arena until 1981, using a couple of his own Buick Regals. He scored two pole positions that year, one top 5 and one top 10. It was a good start and caused more than one team owner to look in his direction. The following year saw Martin field his team for the full schedule, but he came up short to Geoff Bodine for Rookie of the Year honors and short to the bank for the many dollars spent. His only chance to survive was to be a hired gun for aspiring team owners wanting to make it big in the sport.

What followed was bittersweet.

Team owner J. D. Stacy hired Martin in 1983 for what was to be a full schedule of racing. Having a shop full of cars and equipment and nowhere to drive them, Martin sold his operation and set aside the headaches of team ownership to simply drive for a living.

By the seventh event of the season, Martin was fired by Stacy, a move that's still a mystery to some. Martin had finished third at Darlington, South Carolina, when he got the word a change would come after Nashville, Tennessee.

Martin had no choice but to pick up rides wherever possible over the next few years, first with former driver D. K. Ulrich, then in five

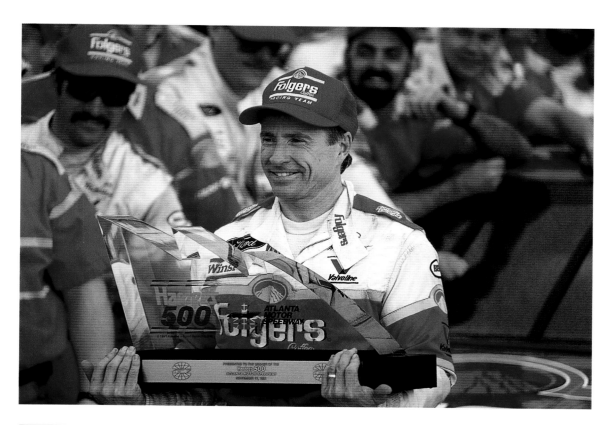

Martin celebrates a win in the final event of the season at Atlanta Motor Speedway held on November 17, 1991. That year the Batesville, Arkansas, driver finished second to Dale Earnhardt in the Winston Cup point standings.

> Long before he was of legal age, he mastered the tracks of the Midwest better than some with twice the experience.

events with Gerry Gunderman, and one event for Roger Hamby. It was a tough existence.

Then came the break of a lifetime.

Automotive engineer Jack Roush was in the midst of forming a Winston Cup team and needed an experienced driver. Martin got word a search was on and convinced Roush to hire him. Money was never a consideration. His only desire was to be back with an established team in Winston Cup competition.

At the start of the 1988 Winston Cup season, Roush hired Martin over a long list of applicants, as he had seen in the few minutes of meeting the Arkansas driver a deep burning desire to win. The first victory came on October 22, 1989, at North Carolina Motor Speedway in Rockingham, North Carolina. Since that first win, Martin and Roush have scored 19 more victories and 29 pole positions and established themselves as winners in the NASCAR Busch Series. A victory in that series in 1987 helped solidify his Winston Cup ride with Roush.

In 1995, Martin scored four victories, one each coming on the short track at North Wilkesboro, North Carolina, the intermediate-sized Charlotte Motor Speedway, the road course at Watkins Glen, New York, and the superspeedway at Talladega, Alabama.

Mark Martin studies the happenings of the garage area at Richmond International Raceway prior to race time on September 12, 1992. He finished second that day.

# EVERETTE DOUGLAS "COTTON" OWENS 1924-

Everette Douglas "Cotton" Owens is best remembered as one of NASCAR's most innovative car owners. His chief concern was his drivers' safety, and he added roll cage bars to the driver's side door before such a rule became mandatory.

Few remember, however, he was once a winning driver in his own right.

Owens was born May 21, 1924, in Union, South Carolina, to Wilson and Etta Owens. With blonde hair as white as the cotton in the fields of Union County, the nickname "Cotton" stuck. The Great Depression kept his family moving from mill town to mill town to keep food on their table and clothes on their back. Families would go for months without the sight of even a dime in the house.

As a youngster, Owens found and fixed a crumpled bicycle and made it functional. He rode that bike to a modified race in Spartanburg's Duncan Park and bought his way in with a quarter, which took months to earn.

Before his 19th birthday in 1943, Owens joined the U.S. Navy and served the country until his discharge a few days before Christmas 1945. It wasn't until the spring of 1946 that Owens first got the bug to drive race cars. While working for an auto body shop in Spartanburg, he and four other very eager racing enthusiasts, Bud Moore, Joe Eubanks, Harold Ballard, and John Tinsley, bought their first car, a 1937 Ford.

Both Moore and Ballard had tried to drive the car but found the venture extremely difficult. Owens hopped aboard, practiced with the car, and turned some good laps. To the surprise of everyone in the group, Owens won the heat race with ease.

When asked what his name was, Owens said he was Bud Moore. He feared his family would be upset over his driving, and he was right. His wife, Dot, who was pregnant with their son, threatened to leave him if he didn't stop driving. But the money began coming in from his short track wins, and with a child on the way, she wasn't about to argue with anything that brought money into the household.

After much success in the modified ranks, Owens couldn't resist the chance to race on NASCAR's Winston Cup (then Grand National) circuit. He won 9 races, finished second 18 times, and earned $65,020 in 158 starts from 1950 through 1964. He ran for the championship only once, but finished second to Lee Petty in 1959.

Owens was known for excellent finishes in modified competition and was called by his peers, "the king of the modifieds." He ran the full-fendered Plymouths throughout the South in conjunction with his big-league efforts. Ironically, the money in the shorter races was more lucrative. For 30 laps of modified racing, Owens got $500 to win. In comparison, 100 laps of Winston Cup competition on the short tracks usually brought in $500.

On September 20, 1964, Owens finished second to Ned Jarrett at Hillsboro, North Carolina, a 0.9-mile dirt track, and put his helmet away for good. He had accomplished what he wanted to accomplish as a driver. End of story. No fanfare. No retirement party. No big deal.

One chapter ended while another much more colorful one was taking shape. Even though the time had come to park his own efforts, there was plenty of administrative fire left in Owens' 5-foot, 6-inch, 140-pound frame. Good things were about to happen.

Owens had begun to back away from driving as early as 1958, having hired Joe Eubanks to drive his car in the Southern 500 that year and also in the 1959 race. Owens had handled the driving everywhere else. The thought of fielding cars instead of driving them was starting to make sense.

In 1960, Bobby Johns drove Owens' cars at Atlanta and Charlotte. He won the Atlanta 500 to give his boss his first superspeedway victory. The next season, drivers Ralph Earnhardt, Marvin Panch, and Fireball Roberts drove his cars in 1961, with Panch and Roberts combining for four victories.

In 1962 and 1963, drivers Junior Johnson, David Pearson, and Billy Wade wheeled his cars, at times in two-car efforts in 1963, but no wins came. By 1964, drivers Earl Balmer, Jim Paschal, and Bobby Isaac joined the list with Owens himself completing his final two events as a driver that year. Pearson ran 61 of 62 events that year and won eight races and 11 pole positions.

With Chrysler's boycott of NASCAR in 1965 due to the ban of the hemi engine, Owens and Pearson went drag racing until the dispute could be settled. The following year, Pearson returned to NASCAR with a vengeance and won the Grand National championship for Owens, collecting 15 victories. On October 16, 1967, the two teamed for their last race, citing disagreements as the cause for the end of their relationship.

Bobby Allison joined Owens after Pearson's departure, but little came of the teaming. Sam McQuagg, Bud Moore (no relation to team owner Bud Moore), Al Unser, Charlie Glotzbach, and Buddy Baker joined Owens. Of those, Glotzbach and Baker gave him the most success. Glotzbach finished consistently in the top-five in select major events. Baker won the 1970 Southern 500, the same weekend Owens was inducted into the National Motorsports Press Association Hall of Fame. Baker also used a Dodge prepared by Owens on March 24 of that year to become the first driver to exceed 200 miles per hour on a closed course at Talladega, Alabama.

Owens last fielded a car in NASCAR competition on October 27, 1973, in the World 600 at Charlotte Motor Speedway with the late Peter Gregg at the controls. Gregg crashed after completing 34 of 400 laps to finish 37th.

Cotton Owens talks with his driver Ralph Earnhardt while at Darlington Raceway for the Rebel 300 held on May 6, 1961. It was Earnhardt's first stint in Winston Cup competition. That day Earnhardt finished seventh after starting sixth.

Owens (6) takes his Pontiac through turns one and two at Darlington Raceway during the Southern 500 held on September 5, 1960. He started 6th and finished 24th.

# BENNY PARSONS 1941-

Although the early years of Benny Parsons' life would be considered hard times by most, the native of Parsonsville, North Carolina, believes they were some of his most memorable years.

Existence was tough, but his great-grandmother and mentor, Julia Parsons, taught him the value of a positive attitude and strong morals. This line of thinking proved invaluable to his racing endeavors. With little excitement going on in the crossroads town, there was also plenty of time to daydream.

Parsons was born July 12, 1941, to Harold and Hazel Parsons. Work around the North Wilkesboro, North Carolina, mountains was scarce during World War II. A slow and exhaustive search turned up nothing and prompted Parsons' father and mother to move to Detroit, Michigan. Young Benny stayed with his great-grandmother, uninterested in leaving his native home.

Life was spent in a clapboard house built around 1890 that didn't have electricity or running water. When he was nine, Parsons went up the hill behind the house and made a reservoir, dug a ditch, and put in a water line to the house, making a system of cold, gravity-fed water.

Parsons also raised chickens and pigs, farmed an acre of land, and kept a cow for milk. If coffee, sugar, or salt was needed, he traded eggs for the luxuries—a standard practice among all of the town's people.

Parsons' parents stayed in touch by phone and letters. During the summer of 1950, Parsons and his great-grandmother made a trip to Detroit, exposing the young lad to televisions, indoor bathrooms, cars, and electricity. Each summer visit, he and his father would spend Friday nights attending races at Motor City Speedway. Detroit was an entirely different world, but Parsons went back to the old house, kerosene lighting, and outhouses.

At 16, he moved away from his clapboard home after helping to build another. After high school and a short stint at North Carolina State University, Parsons eventually moved to Detroit and lived with his parents. He drove a taxi cab on the busy streets of the Motor City, learning the city and meeting people of an entirely different culture.

Parsons married his high school sweetheart, Connie, and moved her to Detroit with him in 1964. That same year, Parsons talked his father into helping him buy a race car. He quickly progressed from landing good finishes

Benny Parsons after wrapping up the 1973 Winston Cup Championship at Rockingham, North Carolina, on October 21, 1973.

to recording race wins. The success he found brought him notice and a small fan following. Being in the home of the three auto makers proved valuable, as being a racer in Detroit seemed to be advantageous.

Down South, racing crashes killed some of Ford's biggest name drivers, such as Joe Weatherly, Fireball Roberts, and Billy Wade. Parsons' name was being passed around a few circles as a good candidate for the Ford team. A meeting with Ford's racing supervisor, Jacques Passino, led Parsons to talk with John Holman of the Holman-Moody racing operation.

---

> Existence was tough, but his great-grandmother and mentor, Julia Parsons, taught him the value of a positive attitude and strong morals. This line of thinking proved invaluable to his racing endeavors.

---

On August 9, 1964, Parsons got a ride from Holman at Asheville-Weaverville Speedway, as did driver Cale Yarborough. Yarborough did well in the race and led several laps, while Parsons had difficulties and spun twice. The ride went to Yarborough, while Parsons went back to Detroit dejected. Ford executives told him if he could run up front in five ARCA events, he could come back and talk. That was his biggest goal of 1965.

Parsons and friend Jon Thorton went to Daytona with a race car to enter in the ARCA 200 the next February. Parsons didn't have a driver's uniform and sent a friend to J. C. Penney's to buy a pair of white size-48 coveralls. A flame-proof solution that was applied to all uniforms made his look horrible. When Parsons won the race three hours later, ARCA officials told him he was a lap down. Speculation was that the uniform looked too bad to photograph in victory lane.

Parsons continued to struggle with his career in February 1969. Ford once again provided a car through Holman, but this time, it was rusted, in pieces, and had to be built from the ground up. It was a test of spirit to see how badly he wanted a good ride on the circuit. Ignoring advice to give up his efforts, Parsons pushed on. As many as 14 friends worked on the car day and night and got the car ready for the long trip to Daytona.

Parsons sat on the pole with the car, but was involved in a crash after suffering a blown tire. To add more stress, his great-grandmother died on November 13 of that year, nine days shy of her 97th birthday.

Ford promised another car for the 1970 ARCA 300, but backed out of the deal, having suffered unrest with future plans concerning NASCAR racing. They pointed him to team owner L. G. DeWitt, which was the most fortunate move of his career. Parsons convinced DeWitt to allow him to race when DeWitt driver Buddy Young was seriously injured at Riverside, California. Soon, Parsons was the team's full-time driver.

With DeWitt, Parsons found the success he had sought. He won the 1973 Winston Cup championship, and in 1975, he captured the Daytona 500 when leader David Pearson spun his Wood Brothers Mercury in the closing laps. The win still ranks as one of the most popular 500 victories in the race's history.

Parsons collected several victories with DeWitt's team. He wheeled cars for Bud Moore, M. C. Anderson, Harry Ranier, Leo Jackson, Rick Hendrick, Junior Johnson, and Junie Donlavey before retiring from driving at the end of the 1990 Winston Cup season with 21 career wins.

Parsons began working in television and radio broadcasting in 1978 and took on the role full time after completing his driving duties.

"Overall, to take my career as a whole, it was really a dream come true. I think that probably in hind sight, I don't think I set my goals high enough.

"I was racing in Detroit and wanted to run in the NASCAR circuit. Once I achieved that, I'm not sure that I didn't feel like my goals were completed. I won a few races which I'm very very thankful for. I think that winning may have become a bigger goal.

"For the first nine years, we always had the monetary restraints. You had to race under those restraints. Money was our restrictor plate. Once I left there, I just didn't set my goals high enough.

"When people come to my house to do filming or come visit or whatever and look around the game room or racing room, the first thing they see is the Winston Cup trophy and that's the one everybody is chasing. I've got one. I didn't get the pot of gold that went with it, but actually, I'm sure Earnhardt doesn't have the gold that came with his seven championships. I'm sure it's gone some place. Really and truly, when it's all said and done, that's about all you have left."

During the final race of the 1973 Winston Cup season at Rockingham, North Carolina, the right side of Parsons' Chevrolet was ripped away in a crash on lap 13.

By patching the car together with scavenged parts, Parsons completed enough laps in his heavily damaged ride to take the 1973 championship.

Parsons stands idle on May 2, 1976, as his crew replaces the engine in his L. G. DeWitt Chevrolet after starting fourth on the grid at the Winston 500 held at Alabama International Motor Speedway.

below: Parsons is in tight company through the fourth turn at Charlotte during the World 600 held May 29, 1977.

Parsons tightens his helmet strap before a race at Darlington Raceway in September 1977.

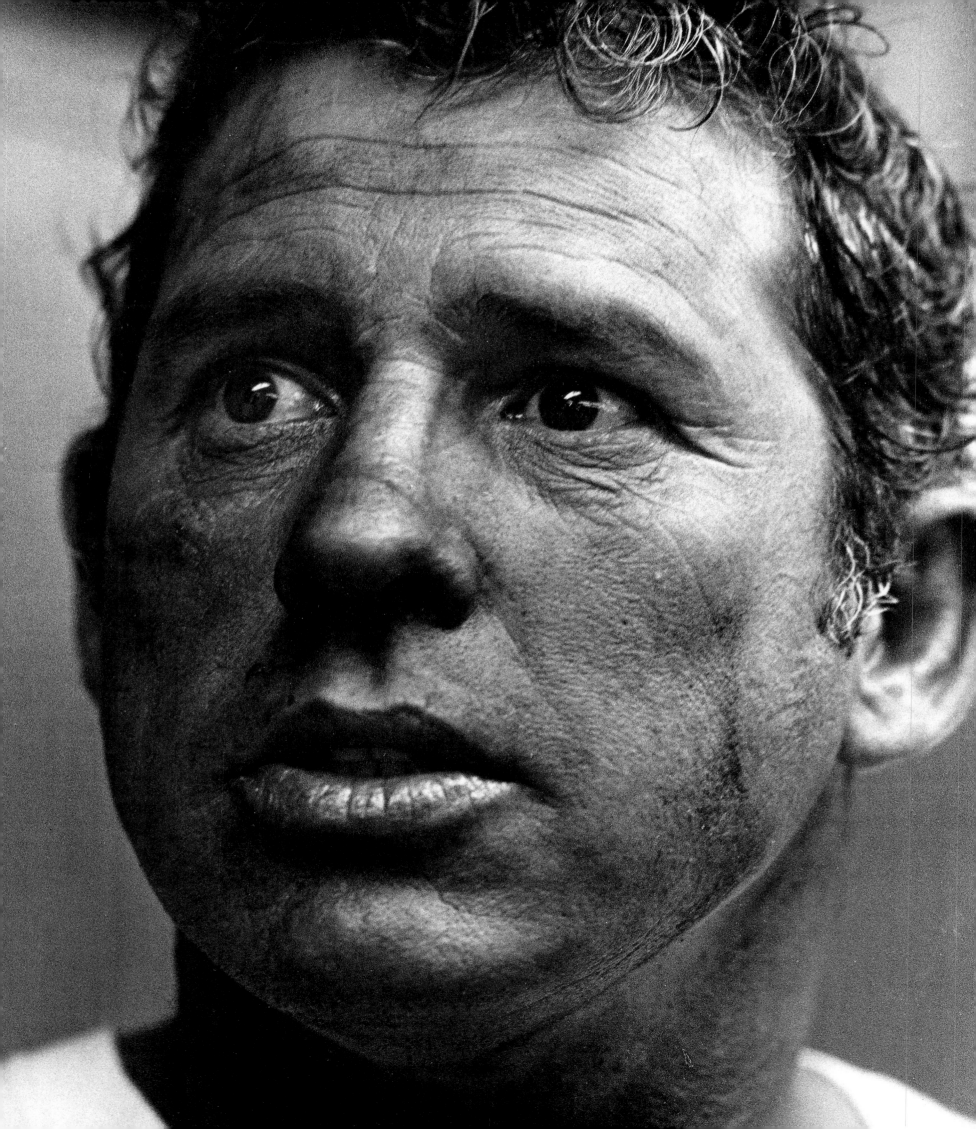

# DAVID PEARSON 1934-

**Y**oung David Pearson had only two aspirations: to drive a wrecker truck and compete in a race car.

He began to fulfill the latter dream when he bought a wrecked 1938 Ford. His mother, Lennie, immediately offered him $30 to get rid of it. He took her money and sold the junk car, netting enough to buy a 1940 Ford. Pearson worked on the car at Mack's restaurant, a local hangout, to keep his mother from finding out about the car. He shaved the heads cut the flywheel, made roll bars from a discarded bed frame, and went racing. His new pastime didn't put much money in his hands, but those few years of low-buck stock car racing fueled his childhood fantasy to drive the big tracks.

When the opportunity to buy an old race car from NASCAR regular Jack Smith had Pearson scrambling for cash, two of his friends started a "David Pearson" fan club on a local radio station. The gag brought money in but not enough to buy the car. Pearson's father, Eura, fronted the $2,000 more that was needed. Suddenly, Pearson was racing in the big leagues. Money was tight, allowing him to only run select races. Still, he emerged as the 1960 Rookie of the Year.

His performance in 1960 landed him an impressive ride in a Pontiac owned by Ray Fox, Sr. It was a big step for a mill town throw back, but Pearson still had to find a job in a heating and roofing company in Spartanburg, South Carolina, to keep money coming in.

Pearson rewarded Fox with wins at the World 600 at Charlotte, the Firecracker 250 at Daytona, and the Dixie 400 at Atlanta. The success brought the attention of the media, who referred to him as "Little David" and "Giant Killer."

His next win came at Richmond, Virginia, in 1964 while driving for Cotton Owens, and he followed that up with seven more victories that year. From the hot mills of South Carolina to the hot sun of victory lane at Daytona, Pearson had traveled a rocky road and accomplished his dreams.

The turbulence created by NASCAR's ban of the Chrysler Hemi engine sent Owens and Pearson to the USAC circuit for much of the 1965 season, but they did return for the superspeedways. That year they grabbed a couple of wins for the record book, and next season there was little stopping them. Pearson reached the pinnacle by winning the 1966 Winston Cup championship.

In 1967, Pearson split the season between Owens and the powerhouse Holman-Moody operation, building static between him and

David Pearson moments after winning the Hickory 250 held on April 3, 1966, at Hickory Speedway in North Carolina while driving a 1964 Dodge for Cotton Owens.

Owens. Pearson eventually left Owens to run Holman-Moody cars. Ironically, his only success that year came through two victories for Owens.

The 1968 season proved to be Pearson's best. In 48 starts for Holman-Moody, he won 16 races and 12 pole positions, as well as his second Winston Cup title. A third championship came in 1969 with 11 wins and 14 poles. The union looked good, but Pearson wanted to back off of running the full schedules. Nineteen starts in 1970 produced only 1 victory and 2 pole positions. In 1971, 10 starts produced 2 wins and 2 pole positions, but John Holman wanted to cut expenses, and to do so, wanted to cut Pearson to virtually nothing as far as race schedules go. A parting of the ways was inevitable.

In a surprise move, Pearson signed a contract with team owner Chris Vallo to drive Pontiacs for the remainder of 1971. His take was $100,000 a year plus a percentage of the winnings. It all looked good on paper, but the purple Pontiac was never competitive. Disputes between Vallo and long-

---

*He shaved the heads, cut the flywheel, made roll bars from a discarded bed frame, and went racing.*

---

time car builder Ray Nichels halted the team before it ever got off the ground. There was little going on for Pearson by the end of the season.

Aside from a one-race deal with Bud Moore and a one-race deal with Junie Donlavey, Pearson had little to fall back on. In the wings was the making of the best ride of his career. Glen Wood had A. J. Foyt in his car but wanted to run the races he selected. Pearson, coming off a limited schedule with Holman-Moody and hardly any schedule with Vallo and Nichels, desperately wanted back in a good ride. By the Rebel 400 at Darlington, South Carolina, on April 16, Pearson was back in full form. He rewarded Wood with a victory in his first attempt with the team. Even though the Wood Brothers routinely ran select events, they were the biggest events, the ones that paid the most money. Pearson liked the sound of that. It was a solid ride, and he knew how competitive Wood Brothers' cars were on superspeedways.

The Pearson-Wood Brothers union was pure magic. Eight seasons produced 43 victories in 143 starts. Their banner year came in 1973 with 11 wins in 18 starts with a then record 10 super-

speedway triumphs in a season. In 1974, there were 7 wins in 19 starts. In 1976, he gave the Wood Brothers their second Daytona 500 victory. They were a tremendous threat each and every time the tour went to a superspeedway.

By 1979, communication between driver and team was beginning to fall apart. During the April 8 Rebel 500 at Darlington, South Carolina, an embarrassing pit stop prompted the break up. Pearson thought he heard "two tires" said on the radio when in reality four tires were to be changed. As the jack dropped with two of the tires still loose, Pearson sped away, only getting as far as the end of pit road before the car was grounded on its left side. By 6:00 p.m. on April 11, Pearson and Wood had decided to part company. Their handshake had lasted for eight glorious seasons.

Once again Pearson was out of a ride, but NASCAR history wasn't yet finished with the "Silver Fox," a nickname given to him early on for his prematurely graying black hair.

When Dale Earnhardt crashed hard at Pocono, Pennsylvania, on July 30, 1979, and was seriously injured, team owner Rod Osterlund called Pearson to fill in for the Southern 500 at Darlington, the sight of the pit miscue five months earlier. Pearson quickly jumped at the chance and won the race, almost as if the track had smiled upon him helping him to forget the nightmare he suffered in the spring race.

Pearson returned to Darlington on April 13, 1980, in a Chevrolet owned by Hoss Ellington and won the Rebel 500 over Benny Parsons. It was his 105th and final victory of his career. Both wins at Darlington proved he still had what it took and did much to erase his shortcomings.

Pearson continued driving until 1986. He retired in April of that year due to recurring back spasms that haunted him throughout his career. Ironically, he was set to drive a Wood Brothers' Ford for injured Neil Bonnett at Charlotte Motor Speedway.

"I had a lot of great years in Winston Cup racing," Pearson says. "Driving was something I really enjoyed doing. I hated to quit when I did, but the back spasms were really starting to bother me.

"I have to say I was real lucky because I never got hurt in a race car. I never broke any bones or had any injuries of any kind. To have a long career without some type of injury is rare, but I never had one in 25 years of racing.

"Of all the teams I drove for, I'd say the Wood Brothers were the very best to me. We had some real good years together, and we are still best of friends today. They are class people."

After a long afternoon of chasing Cale Yarborough in the Southern 500, Pearson finished a close second on September 2, 1968.

There was no stopping Pearson on March 9, 1969, at Rockingham, North Carolina. Here he works his way through turn one at North Carolina Motor Speedway, eventually winning the race in Holman-Moody's first Talladega Torino.

Pearson in September 1977 at the Rebel 500.

Pearson stops his Holman-Moody Ford for some fast pit work at Charlotte on May 26, 1968. Driver Dick Hutcherson hands Pearson a cold drink.

Pearson's role after his retirement in 1986 was to field his own team for sons Larry, Ricky, and Eddie.

# KYLE PETTY 1960-

**B**eing the son of the King of Stock Car Racing leaves little or nothing to the imagination where career choices are concerned. It was a natural progression for Kyle Petty to follow right in the footsteps of his famous father, Richard, no question about it. He was set to become the third-generation Petty stock car driver, set to break his father's records as well as everyone else's; set to become NASCAR's biggest and brightest star.

The newspapers touted his talents even before he drove a race car. They were sure he would be a chip off the old block. He was the talk of racing circles, both foreign and abroad. A born success, they would say.

That's where expectation and reality collide head on. To become a NASCAR Winston Cup driver was a tough but reasonable goal for Kyle Petty. To meet the expectation of the press and public and become the best of the best was a much different story.

The warnings from the family were true: The road would be filled with many obstacles. As with anyone born-into-celebrity status, every move is dissected and analyzed.

As a child, the younger Petty looked at stock car racing as nothing more than his father's profession. The cars in the nearby shop were shiny blue, carried painted numbers on their doors, and were set up to be turned left around short tracks and superspeedways. Petty grew up surrounded by the sounds of air grinders hitting metal and engines screaming on the dynamometer.

Although go-carts were out of the question in the Petty home, Kyle was allowed to start driving the family car at age 12. He'd spend countless hours driving down the long dirt driveway, along the two-lane road to the home of Uncle Maurice, into his driveway, and back the other direction. Kyle was going around in circles—at a reduced pace—just as his father, Richard, and grandfather, Lee, did before him.

From the driveway, Petty graduated to sporadic trips to the corner store, that is, until the Randolph County (North Carolina) Sheriff's Department brought him home to mother with numerous warnings about driving without a license.

Petty was quite adventurous as a teenager, finding trouble at every turn. He wasn't beyond passing stray dogs through wet concrete or crashing his grandfather's brand new riding lawn mower into an oak tree.

When he could behave himself, music and his athletics showcased his talents. There were

Petty receives some advice from his father before the ARCA 200 at Daytona held on February 17, 1979. Petty won the race in his first start as a driver.

> The newspapers touted his talents even before he drove a race car. They were sure he would be a chip off the old block. He was the talk of racing circles, both foreign and abroad.

many topics that held his interest, and he was extremely involved in all of them.

As expected, Petty traded all his whimsical ideas for a career driving stock cars. Knowing the pressures he would face because of the legacy left before him, he was tested. His seriousness about the sport had to be dead on the mark or he would fail.

At the start of Speedweeks in 1979, Petty came to Daytona International Speedway with a Dodge Magnum, a discarded Winston Cup machine his father used the year before with no success. Even though it came with a heavy box-like design, it was perfect for the younger Petty, who entered it in ARCA competition.

Miraculously, young Petty won the ARCA 200, his first outing on a closed course. For a brief time, he was the only undefeated stock car driver in America. Two days later, father Richard won his seventh-career Daytona 500 in dramatic fashion.

His career launched, a total of 169 Cup races passed before Petty found victory lane

in Winston Cup competition; doing so with the Wood Brothers team at the Richmond, Virginia, short track in 1986. The win marked him as the first third-generation driver to win a Winston Cup race. His grandfather, Lee, won his first race in 1949, and his father, Richard, first stood on the top spot in 1960. Kyle notched another win the following year at the prestigious Coca-Cola 600, his first superspeedway triumph.

Six more wins followed with team owner Felix Sabates, but the Cuban transplant and the North Carolina country boy elected to part ways in 1996 after eight seasons together. The two had become as close as father and son, but the results on the track simply didn't warrant another year together.

Petty has come full circle, driving his own Pontiacs, co-owned with his father and David Evans to form what is known as pe2. His quest is to perform consistently in Winston Cup racing, casting aside those ridiculous expectations placed upon him long ago.

The playful child continues to come out by way of his Harley Davidson motorcycle, love for the music of the late Elvis Presley, and building sand castles at the beach. Petty will most likely never top his father's accomplishments, but that's just fine with him. All he wants to be is himself.

Kyle Petty enjoys the spoils of victory after winning the World 600 on May 24, 1987, for the Wood Brothers.

# RICHARD PETTY 1937-

At 14 years of age, Richard Petty was content to help build engines for his father's race cars and to turn a few warm-up laps now and then. Those prerace rides fueled a deeply imbedded desire to embark on his own driving career. By the time he finished driving, his name was at the top of the win list with nearly twice as many career victories as any other competitor.

His father, Lee Petty, first began driving stock cars in 1947 at 33 years of age and won NASCAR championships in 1954, 1958, and 1959. His sons, Richard and Maurice, spent their late teenage years maintaining their father's cars until they were old enough to legally turn a steering wheel of their own. Eventually, Maurice, known as "Chief," elected to spend time turning wrenches and building awesome engines, leaving the driving to Richard.

Those early powerplants were so good that the sheriff's department of Randolph County, North Carolina, had the Pettys build their squad car engines.

The Petty dynasty started in a 20-by-25-foot shed held up by cedar poles. Next to it was a large board nailed between two trees that was used to butcher hogs.

Petty first drove a stock car on July 12, 1958, in a 100-mile Convertible event where he finished sixth. His first NASCAR Winston Cup (then Grand National) event came at the Canadian National Exposition Speedway in Toronto, Canada, on July 18, 1958. His father, Lee, won the race, with the 21-year old Petty 17th in the 19-car field after hitting the fence in the 55th lap. Petty's first win came on February 28, 1960, at the Charlotte (North Carolina) Fairgrounds over drivers Rex White and Doug Yates. It was the beginning of a long illustrious career.

On February 23, 1964, Petty won his first superspeedway event at the Daytona 500 and went on to record his first Winston Cup (then Grand National) championship, all coming at the young age of 26. The win came in part due to the use of a 2-by-4 bolted to the side of the seat to keep Petty from sliding around at 190 miles per hour. In 61 starts that year, he found victory lane

nine times and amassed more than $114,000 in winnings. NASCAR had found a new star.

With Chrysler's hemi engine banned from competition at the start of the 1965 season, the Petty family went drag racing with Richard at the controls. The results were disastrous, and by July 25 Chrysler was back in NASCAR in force. The Pettys were back in the stock car racing business, not a day too soon.

There were eight wins logged in 1966, but the following year, Petty was the dominant force. In 48 starts, he won 27 races, 10 of which were consecutive, as well as his second championship. He added four more championships, beginning in 1971 with 21 wins in 46 starts, 1972 with 8 wins in 31 starts, 1974, and in 1975 with 23 wins in 60 starts. Add another in 1979 and Petty has a coveted collection of seven

---

**He is a living legend who has won on every speedway used in NASCAR and quite a few no longer on the tour.**

---

championships. Only Dale Earnhardt has equaled that number in NASCAR competition. Until Earnhardt came onto the scene in 1979, Petty was virtually untouchable in the category of champion.

Not all was diamonds and gold. Petty suffered several racing injuries as well as severe stomach problems in the late 1970s. In October 1983, tension at Petty Enterprises reached an all-time high just after Petty logged his 198th victory. Under the hood of his Pontiac was an oversized engine, much bigger than the 358-cubic-inch allowed by NASCAR. Built by brother Maurice, it measured 381.983 cubic inches in postrace inspection. Also, Petty had left side tires on the right side of the car, which was against NASCAR rules at the time. The victory was allowed to remain in the record books, but Petty was fined $35,000 and had 104 Win-

ston Cup points taken from the 1983 standings.

Petty finished the season with his own operation but elected to join former team owner Mike Curb, leaving the family operation for the first time in his career. Son Kyle Petty was left to handle the driving duties for the team. Petty recorded win number 199 at Dover, Delaware, on May 20, 1984. Just over a month later, on July 4, win number 200 came at Daytona International Speedway, a track where Petty had enjoyed so much success. His closest rival in the win column is David Pearson with 105.

Petty returned to Petty Enterprises in 1986, but no more victories were recorded. His final event came on November 15, 1992, where he started 35th and finished 39th amid much fanfare after completing a season-long fan appreciation tour.

Petty continues to oversee Petty Enterprises. Drivers Rick Wilson, Wally Dallenbach, John Andretti, and Bobby Hamilton have handled the driving duties since Petty retired. Of those, Hamilton put No. 43 back in victory lane at Phoenix, Arizona, on October 27, 1996.

Thousands of times throughout his 34-year career, Petty has been referred to as "The King." With 200 career Winston Cup victories in 1,185 starts, he is arguably NASCAR's number one driver throughout its 50-year history.

Underneath his patented smile, mustache, sunglasses, and black cowboy hat with feathered band, Petty is one of the most recognized personalities in all of motorsports. He has enjoyed overwhelming racing success while remaining available to his millions of fans, almost as if each one is a relative he's meeting for the first time. His easy personality had done more for the growth of NASCAR than any other facet in the sport. He is a living legend who has won on every speedway used in NASCAR and quite a few no longer on the tour.

Talking about winning the 1964 Daytona 500, Petty summed up his career nicely. "That was the first superspeedway race I'd ever won," Petty says fondly between smiles. "And it was a big, big deal. But every race I ever won has been a big deal as far as I'm concerned."

Richard Petty at the Budweiser 500 on May 31, 1992. The race was held in Dover, Delaware.

Petty's first superspeedway victory came at the Daytona 500 held on February 23, 1964. Before season's end, he captured his first of seven Winston Cup championships.

With the customary wet cloth clenched between his teeth, Petty makes his way down the front stretch at Atlanta Motor Speedway on April 2, 1967. He finished 22nd after blowing an engine.

left: Chiropractor David Farlowe from High Point, North Carolina, gives Petty a rub-down before the World 600 in Charlotte, North Carolina, in the late 1960s.

Petty waters himself down with a water hose just before a hot Atlanta race held on April 2, 1967. He started 22nd and finished 2nd.

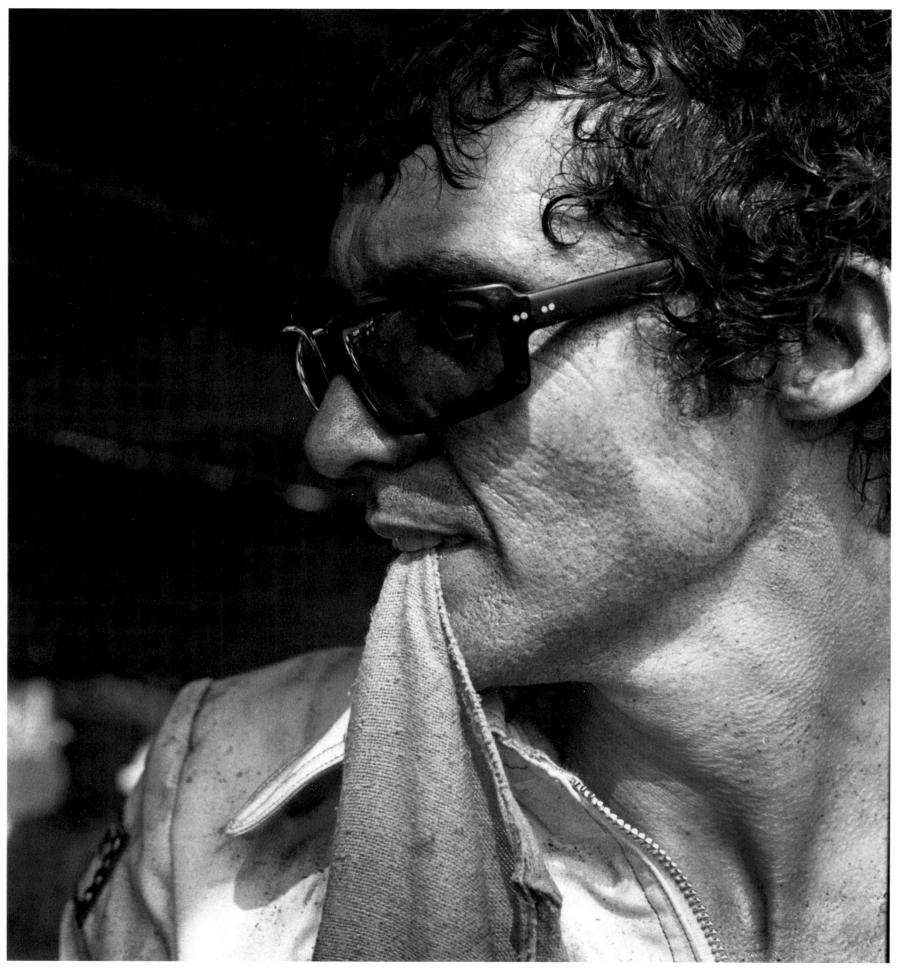

Petty makes a pit stop late on February 18, 1979, in the Daytona 500 before logging his sixth career victory in NASCAR's biggest event.

left: Petty after a long, hot May 4 at Talladega in 1975.

At Darlington Raceway on September 11, 1977, Petty takes in some oxygen after Dave Marcis took over as a relief driver.

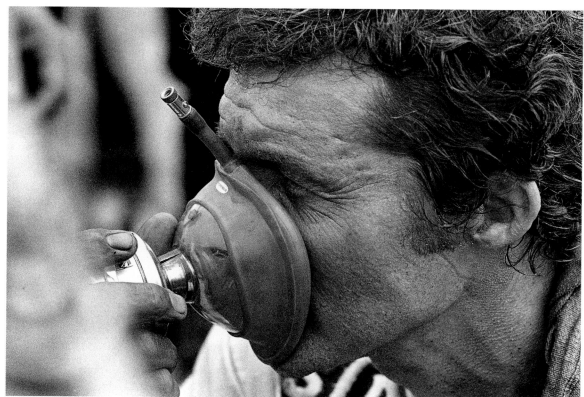

# TIM RICHMOND 1955-1989

Strong willed and charismatic, Tim Richmond's good looks and take-no-prisoners driving style gave him a large following of fans. In seven short years in NASCAR Winston Cup racing, he made everlasting impressions, both through racing victories and black controversy. Women adored him. AIDS eventually killed him.

Born June 7, 1955, Richmond carried a crazy streak within him from early childhood, as he wasn't past doing anything, no matter how outlandish the stunt may seem. It was the fuel he needed to later drive virtually anything on wheels. He worked his way through the Sprint Car, Supermodified, and Mini-Indy divisions, emerging onto the Indy car scene in 1980. That year, he competed in the Indianapolis 500 and was the media's idol for the entire month of May. In the Indy 500, he was running in the top five when he ran out of fuel and had to pull to the inside of the speedway. His ninth-place finish earned him Rookie of the Year honors. At race's end, winner Johnny Rutherford stopped and picked up Richmond, who was walking back to the pits.

Just after the Indy 500 start, Richmond picked up a Winston Cup ride through Pocono International Raceway owner and president Joe Mattiolli. His debut started in 23rd and resulted in 12th. Richmond immediately fell in love with stock cars. Never again did he go for open wheel racing. It was the first of five races he ran with former team owner D. K. Ulrich.

Richmond possessed the talent and personality to get himself noticed. In 1981, he competed in 29 events for four different car owners, Ulrich, Kennie Childres, Bob Rogers, and Rahmoc Enterprises. There were some impressive runs that caught the eye of fellow competitors and team owners alike. By the start of the following year, he had landed his first good ride, first with the "big promise-little results" outfit owned by Mike Lovern and later hooked up with J. D. Stacy for 25 starts. On June 6, 1982, Richmond finished second to Bobby Allison at Pocono, Pennsylvania, after a very strong performance. The next week, he was in his first Winston Cup event on the road course at Riverside, California, over Terry Labonte. His arrival was simply waiting for a stage on which to happen.

In 1983, Richmond attracted the eye of drag racer Raymond Beadle, who was fielding a Winston Cup effort on the side. He was twice successful during the 1983 and 1984 seasons,

but also showed a hot temper at some of NASCAR's rulings.

In 1985, Richmond found himself at odds with Dale Earnhardt at both Bristol, Tennessee, and Martinsville, Virginia. Heated words over Earnhardt's driving tactics showed a different side of the Ashland, Ohio, native. It was his first exposure to good ol' fashioned southern stock car racing, but Richmond wasn't amused.

Auto dealer Rick Hendrick tapped Richmond to drive his Chevrolets in 1986, giving him a new lease on his driving career. The beard and long hair he sported in 1985 became a thing of the past. He shaved off the beard, got stylish haircuts, and began dressing in the finest designer suits. It was the start of the new Tim Richmond.

The press touted the Richmond-Hendrick-Hyde combination as potent going into the 1986 season. For the first half of the season, however, the match between Richmond and Harry Hyde worked about as well as fire and

---

*Richmond carried a crazy streak within him from early childhood, as he wasn't past doing anything, no matter how outlandish the stunt may seem. It was the fuel he needed to drive virtually anything on wheels.*

---

water. It was rebellious youth against conservative aged experienced. Defiance was the name of Richmond's game at every turn. While Hyde was trying to save transmissions and tires, Richmond was jamming gears and burning tread. Hyde got in Richmond's face more than once. It was like talking to a brick wall.

Finally, during a tire test at North Wilkesboro, North Carolina, Hyde talked Richmond into driving 50 laps his way and 50 laps Richmond's way. At the end of the test, Hyde calculated that driving with Richmond's usual abandonment would put him as much as seven laps down from a more consistent pace at the end of a 400-lap race. That got Richmond's attention.

Their entire relationship was considered as the basis of the motion picture, *Days of Thunder,* starring Tom Cruise and Robert Duvall.

In the summer heat, Richmond and Hyde proceeded to burn up the circuit. From June 8

through September 7, 1986, they won six races, finished second twice, sixth once, and fifteenth also once. He won seven of the last seventeen races, finishing out the season with another win at Riverside, California. He was voted co-winner of the National Motorsports Press Association Driver of the Year after finishing third in the Winston Cup point standings, sharing the honor with 1986 champion Dale Earnhardt.

Even though all was going well on the track, Richmond was fighting a quiet personal battle. People began to notice that he didn't look well, and immediately after winning the final event of the season at Riverside, Richmond checked into the Cleveland Clinic with double pneumonia. It was the beginning of the end of an outstanding Winston Cup career.

It wasn't until May that Richmond returned to racing, coming to the Winston special non-points event as a spectator. He did test his car at Darlington, South Carolina, and Rockingham, North Carolina, turning impressive speeds each time.

On June 14, 1987, Richmond returned to Pocono, Pennsylvania, and took the lead over Bill Elliott with 47 laps remaining. The win was a tearful, joyful return for Richmond, Hyde, the crew, and virtually every fan in attendance. Miraculously, Richmond was victorious at Riverside on June 21 and recorded his last career win.

When the tour got to Watkins Glen International and Michigan Speedway in August, drivers registered complaints that they couldn't safely drive with him. At Michigan, he was awakened in his private bus minutes before he was to qualify his Chevrolet. By September 9, 1987, Richmond resigned from Hendrick Motorsports.

Richmond was battling the effects of AIDS, but did not reveal his disease to the public. It is believed he discovered he had the disease while in the Cleveland Clinic.

Richmond attempted to drive in the Busch Clash of 1988, but NASCAR suspended him indefinitely, citing he had failed a pre-race physical drug test. Prior to going to Daytona, he took a drug test to ensure the AZT he was taking would not show up. The drug test had been falsified by NASCAR, as they had attempted to keep his AIDS quiet. Richmond was tested again, and the result was negative. Richmond sued for $20 million but settled out of court in January 1989.

Richmond died on August 13, 1989, from the complications of AIDS. In 185 starts, he collected 13 victories, 14 pole positions, and $2,310,018 in career winnings.

Tim Richmond after winning the 300-mile Busch Series event at Charlotte held in May 1986.

# GLENN "FIREBALL" ROBERTS 1929-1964

Glenn "Fireball" Roberts found his life's calling partly by geographic location. He grew up in and around Daytona Beach. The area's legacy of speed naturally fueled his desire to drive fast on some of the world's most famous sand.

The nickname "Fireball" came long before he ever drove a stock car. His lightning-fast softball pitching for the Zellwood Mud Hens American Legion team gave him quite a reputation on the local fields near his Tavares, Florida, home. That nickname defined his life and, ironically, the means of his death.

Even though he was gaining a reputation for his stellar driving ability in modified competition, the publicity shy Roberts hated the thought of having to go before the public to explain his good finishes. He kept to himself and longed to be away from those who wanted a piece of his growing popularity. The fact he was a loner kept all but a select few from getting to know him. Roberts wanted a piece of the limelight without interference in his private life.

His auto racing debut came on August 5, 1947, at North Wilkesboro (North Carolina) Speedway. He enjoyed the modified ranks and would race seven days a week.

His debut in a NASCAR-sanctioned event took place at the Edward Rayson Memorial modified race held on February 15, 1948, at Daytona. Only 12 drivers finished the wreck-filled 150-lap race on the 2.2-mile circuit of sand and asphalt. Roberts only completed nine laps before he missed the south turn and ended up in the surf.

Roberts' first NASCAR-sanctioned win came on August 13, 1950, at Hillsboro, North Carolina, his third race on the tour. Three weeks later, he finished second in the prestigious Southern 500 at Darlington (South Carolina) Raceway and was dubbed an up-and-coming star by the media.

Despite the high expectations generated by his promising start, Roberts went winless for the next six years. Five wins came in 1956 with his first Ford factory effort provided by Pete DePaolo. He won eight races in 1957, five of them with DePaolo and three more while driving his own cars.

The 1958 season was his year. Teamed with Atlanta businessman Frank Strickland and crew chief Paul McDuffie, he was virtually unstoppable. He won several races that year in both the NASCAR Convertible and Grand National divisions, including the prestigious Southern 500 at Darlington. He was 14th in the Convertible division point standings and 11th in the Grand National ranks. To top off his season, he was voted Professional Athlete of the Year by the Florida Sportswriters Association, the first time a race car driver was awarded the honor.

---

> Roberts hated the thought of having to go before the public to explain his good finishes. He kept to himself and longed to be away from those who wanted a piece of his growing popularity.

---

His arrival as a superstar couldn't have come at a better time, as the Daytona International Speedway was set to open in February 1959.

Even though Roberts was successful with Strickland and McDuffie, Roberts couldn't refuse an offer to drive factory-backed Pontiacs for team owner Jim Stephens and crew chief Henry "Smokey" Yunick. The factory Pontiac should have been first class. Oddly, he entered the Pontiac in only four events that year and picked up rides with other owners. The deal wasn't as sweet as first believed. All told, Roberts won only one race during the 44-race season, the inaugural Firecracker 250 at Daytona, which he won driving the Stephens Pontiac.

Roberts won twice in 1960 and seven times in 1961. His biggest triumph was winning the 1962 Daytona 500. He sweetened the pot that weekend by a victory in one of two 125-mile qualifying races and securing the pole position while driving for Stephens and chief mechanic Yunick. The victory moved Roberts closer to becoming a legend in stock car racing circles.

Roberts scored four more victories in 1963 in only 20 starts, including, again, the Southern 500 at Darlington. It was one of his most enjoyable years, but it was his last complete season of racing. He would race only eight more times before a tragic accident would occur.

Roberts was burned badly in an accident at Charlotte on May 24, 1964. On the seventh lap of the World 600, Roberts' Ford made contact with Junior Johnson's Ford, sending Roberts hard into the inside retaining wall, where his car exploded in flames. He was rescued by fellow driver Ned Jarrett and spent nearly six weeks in a Charlotte hospital.

The flames took an especially severe toll on Roberts, due to the fact that his driving suit was not flame retardant. Roberts battled asthma, and the smell of the NASCAR-mandated fire retardant solution caused problems with his breathing and irritated his skin. Through a written report from his doctor, NASCAR had granted him permission to drive wearing a cotton uniform not treated with a fire-retardant solution.

Despite the severe burns, Roberts' condition was improving until complications from pneumonia, swelling of his lungs, blood poisoning, and infection set in. He died just after 7:00 A.M. on July 2, 1964.

"Glen was a very intense person," says Doris Roberts. "My husband believed in the NASCAR organization. He really enjoyed his career and all the things he was able to accomplish.

"One area he was really good at was qualifying. He was a good qualifier and put a lot of emphasis on that. He liked it because his name would be mentioned more prominently in the newspapers.

"We all loved him and miss him still today."

Junior Johnson (left) talks with Fireball Roberts before the start of the National 400 held on October 14, 1962. Johnson won the race with Roberts finishing second.
*Charlotte Motor Speedway*

A young Roberts poses with driver Buddy Shuman early in their careers. Once when a reporter asked Shuman how to get around Darlington, Shuman replied, "I take the car down the straightaways, and Lord Calvert takes her through the turns." *Buddy Shuman Collection*

On March 20, 1963, Roberts goes to the Holman-Moody Ford operation to check out his new powerhouse ride.

Roberts (22) starts from pole position and leads the field at Asheville-Weaverville (North Carolina) Speedway. Roberts finished 18th on that July 1, 1956, after a blown tire.

Roberts wheels his Holman-Moody Ford to a 10th-place finish in the World 600 held on June 2, 1963.

# RICKY RUDD 1956-

**F**ull of competitive spirit, Ricky Rudd knew from an early age stock car racing would fit him like a glove.

His youthful face has been seen in victory lane at least once per season for the past 14 consecutive years. In 1986 and 1987, Rudd logged two victories each season while driving for Bud Moore, bringing his total win count to 17.

Rudd began racing motocross and go-carts at a very early age and didn't drive a stock car until he first sat down in a Winston Cup car in 1975. In four starts that year with the late Bill Champion, a top 10 finish was indicative of his talent and potential.

In 1976, Rudd entered four more events in cars fielded by his father, Al Rudd, Sr. He reeled off several top-10 finishes, a hint at the consistency that would mark Rudd's career. The family tackled the majority of the schedule in 1977, and Rudd earned Rookie of the Year honors that season.

> Rudd began racing motocross and go-carts at a very early age and didn't drive a stock car until he first sat down in a Winston Cup car in 1975.

Rudd entered 13 races in 1978 with results sufficient to land a ride with long-time team owner Junie Donlavey for the full schedule in 1979. He scored two third-place finishes and three fifths and earned nearly $150,000. Overall, it was a good learning season for Rudd.

In 1980, racing with his family operation for 13 events, Rudd was in a make-or-break situation. Money was running out quickly and one good race could get him noticed by the more highly financed teams on the circuit. A solid finish would provide his only chance to remain an active driver.

Rudd entered the National 500 at Charlotte Motor Speedway in October with a year-old car and qualified on the outside front row. By race's end, Rudd was fourth behind Dale Earnhardt, Cale Yarborough, and Buddy Baker. The impressive run got him noticed by several veteran team owners.

Ricky Rudd shows the strain of 500 miles after a May 6, 1979, event at Talladega, Alabama.

Rudd signed with Digard Racing and replaced Darrell Waltrip for the 1981 season. Waltrip vacated the high-profile ride to drive for Junior Johnson. Even though the results from the Digard-Rudd union weren't overly impressive, there were definite signs of promise.

Rudd joined the Richard Childress team in 1982 and won his first Winston Cup event at Riverside, California, the next year. Rudd won six races driving for Bud Moore, two more with Kenny Bernstein, four more wins and a second-place finish in the Winston Cup point championship in 1990 with Rick Hendrick, and five more victories with his own

Rudd scored the biggest win at his career at the 1997 Brickyard 400, where a strong run kept him within striking distance and crafty pit strategy in the last few laps brought home the win. *Stephen Baker*

team through August 2, 1997. Along with his wins have come 23 pole positions and nearly $12 million in career earnings.

"Winston Cup racing is the only thing I ever wanted to do," Rudd says. "I've had a very rewarding career and really enjoy fielding my own cars now. What I'm doing in the '90s is building my team for some good things to come in the future."

# KEN SCHRADER 1955-

At three years of age, Ken Schrader knew his life would be going around in circles. His father, the late Bill Schrader, a former racer himself, placed a truck axle in the ground and secured it at a vertical angle with concrete. A few days after the foundation was dry, the elder Schrader attached one end of a 20-foot cable to the pole and the other end to a go-cart. Thus, a new career was born.

Young Kenny would strap himself into the go-cart, push the throttle, and turn left in a circle until he ran out of gas. Over and over, he ran his cart—that is, until the tires were nearly burned off the wheels or one of numerous clutches failed.

As he got older, Schrader walked the three-eighths of a mile down the road to his father's short track, Lake Hill Speedway in Valley Park, Missouri. He practiced flagging the race cars as they came through the gate or stood in his front yard and gave them the green flag as they passed by.

Schrader raced go-carts at age 3, quarter midgets by 5, and motorcycles by the time he was 10 years old. In 1971, he won his first track championship in Hobby Class cars at the ripe old age of 16.

Schrader didn't own a trailer to carry his cars. His solution was to look both directions on the public road and drive his race car down to the family track. After two years and countless races, the Missouri Highway Patrol never caught on to his form of race car transportation.

---

> Young Kenny would strap himself into the go-cart, push the throttle, and turn left in a circle until he ran out of gas.

---

He competed in various short-track events in a number of divisions, collecting hundreds of victories around the Midwest. The success he enjoyed gave him a lot of headlines, thus paving the way for a more lucrative career.

The itch to drive in NASCAR Winston Cup competition became great by the early 1980s. In 1984, Schrader joined the late Elmo Langley, a longtime Winston Cup competitor who had finally vacated his driver's seat for more youthful talent. The following year, Schrader joined Junie Donlavey for three full seasons where he scored several top 10 finishes.

While working miracles with limited financing, Schrader caught the eye of team owner Rick Hendrick. During their nine-year relationship, they collected four victories and 14 pole positions in 267 starts. A dream that started as a cable hooked to an axle has earned Schrader nearly $9 million in his career.

During their tenure, in 1989 and 1990, Schrader won the Busch Clash, a special non-points event for pole position winners held annually at Daytona International Speedway. He also won the pole position for the Daytona 500 three years running in 1988, 1989, and 1990.

Near the end of 1996, Schrader parted company with Hendrick, both citing the need to try their hands elsewhere: Schrader with another team and Hendrick with another driver. Andy Petree, a former crew chief with team owners Leo Jackson and Richard Childress, purchased Jackson's team and hired Schrader for the 32-race schedule.

"I've enjoyed a great career, both on the short tracks and with NASCAR Winston Cup racing," Schrader says. "Man, I like to race more than anything else I do. I've done nothing else in my life. Racing is really important to me. I just want to win more races. With Andy Petree's team, I'm sure those wins will come. There's still time to get a few more."

Ken Schrader enjoys victory lane ceremonies on February 12, 1989, after winning the Busch Clash special non-points event for pole-position winners.

Schrader takes his Hendrick Motorsports Chevrolet down the front chute at Rockingham, North Carolina, en route to a 10th-place finish.

# WENDELL SCOTT 1921-1990

On an out-of-the-way shelf in the home of his widow, Mary, rests a cherished trophy earned by the late Wendell Scott.

Made of stained wood and thickly varnished, it's symbolic of the entire career of a black man who attempted to break down racial barriers in the deep South in the 1960s, often times at more than 190 miles per hour. Having suffered through a NASCAR career of strife and unrest, Scott is remembered for his sacrifices and willingness to continue when all odds were against him.

Through his efforts on short tracks and super speedways alike, he won just more than $180,000 in 500 career starts.

Ignored by many are his 200 victories on tracks around his Danville, Virginia, home, which propelled him to try his hand at the bigger, more recognized arenas of the Winston Cup (then Grand National) circuit.

That little brown excuse for a trophy in his widow's house marks his only big-league stock car victory, coming in 1964 on a small dirt track in Jacksonville, Florida.

For Scott, the quest to follow those of his color into the limelight of professional sports meant such humiliating experiences as traveling to races at night when the harrassment was light, the inability to buy a simple hot dog at concession stands where he raced, and having to buy groceries from the back door of stores. There was always the need to stand guard over his race car so others had no chance to sabotage his efforts before he attempted qualifying runs.

The sole win came amid a supposed scoring controversy. Reportedly, once the official beauty queen (who was white) was told she must kiss a black man in victory lane, she ran from the premises. To ensure those in the stands wouldn't riot because of the outcome, Buck Baker was awarded the win on the spot. But a month later a scoring "check" gave Scott the win. It was made official in a quiet, private ceremony where there was little glory and very little fortune. The small wooden trophy was given to him accompanied by the staccato of the local press' flashbulbs. Nothing more.

Scott was hated by many fellow drivers simply because he was an African American who wanted a piece of a white man's

Scott fought prejudice, humiliation, and dirty tricks to continue to compete in the sport he loved.

> Scott stared at the other driver through the driver's side window opening and pointed a handgun in his direction. Never again did the antagonist bother Scott.

world. Drivers constantly put him and his far less superior equipment into the wall; but with a display of class, he kept quiet and would not be intimidated. He came back week after week, simply out of courage and a love of stock car racing. Only once did he have to silence a long-time critic, who confronted him with blood in his eye and a fight on his mind.

As the two drivers passed through one of the flat turns circling the football field at Bowman Gray Stadium, the offender rammed his car into Scott's Chevrolet, as if attempting to knock him off the race track. Scott stared at the other driver through the driver's side window opening and pointed a handgun in his direction. Never again did the antagonist bother Scott.

Scott's career ended in 1973 after he suffered life-threatening injuries in the early stages of a 500-mile event on the high banks of Talladega Superspeedway. With his body old beyond its years after many seasons of hard competition and living and possessing a wrecked race car that carried a note from the bank, Scott tearfully said good-bye to a sport that had treated him like an intruder.

Scott died on December 22, 1990, after a long bout with spinal cancer. Before his death, a major motion picture was made on his life with actor Richard Pryor in the lead role.

Wendell Scott shows the look of determination that got him into NASCAR racing. His 1961 Chevrolet is in the background.

Usually having limited help, Scott would often exit his race car and service it during the race.

Scott makes some last minute adjustments to the rear of his battle-scarred Ford.

Scott returns to North Carolina Motor Speedway for a visit in 1985.

One of Scott's best rides was provided by Richard Howard on May 28, 1972, for the World 600 at Charlotte Motor Speedway. Scott started 11th and finished 22nd.

# CURTIS TURNER 1924-1970

If one of the endless stream of parties Curtis Turner held at his home in Charlotte, North Carolina showed the slightest sign of getting dull, he would stand up, turn off the stereo, and announce, "All right folks, there will be a new party starting in 10 minutes!"

Turner was the true definition of a wild buck in the woods. Racing folklore places him in more precarious positions than possibly any other race driver in history. Turner lived from minute to minute, throwing caution to the wind. His exploits off the track were as legendary as those on. Death finally found him, and stories concerning his death are still inconclusive.

Aside from the wild parties where anything would be commonplace, Turner's most famous off-track escapade occurred in the early 1960s. While idle from the yet another loss of his driver's license, Turner usually looked to his trusty airplane for transportation.

While flying over Easely, South Carolina, Turner spotted a friend's house below. There was no question the friend would have his favorite libation waiting for him, so Turner decided to literally drop in for a drink. Turner sat the twin-engine plane down on the street, ducking just below the power and telephone lines.

A few drinks later, he and his friend remembered the plane outside and rushed to move it before the police made their Sunday rounds. Upon takeoff, the local Baptist church was just letting out its Sunday service. Turner got the plane off the ground, but the tail snagged the power lines, ripping them off the poles.

Turner thought little of the incident until he landed at the Charlotte airport. A Federal Aviation Administration representative held out his hand to collect Turner's pilot's license as he stepped off the plane. Despite efforts from his lawyers, Turner was grounded for years. Still, an occasional airplane found him at the controls.

Turner was born April 12, 1924, in the Shenandoah Mountains of Floyd, Virginia. Lumber was his family's source of income, and from his early days of waking up to the smell of fresh cut pine, Turner had logging in his blood. By the time he was 20, he had built his business into a prosperous operation. It would be the first of several fortunes he would make in his 46 years. He possessed an uncanny ability for estimating amounts of board feet that tracts of land carried simply by flying over them in his plane.

While not running the lumber business, Turner spent time in what he once called "a shine clan." On occasion, those moonshiners would stage backwoods races, events akin to cockfighting in the sense that word of mouth was the only form of advertising.

In one of those events, Turner took an old 1940 Ford and put it out front, all the while making his car fit in what seemed to be openings half its size. He crashed hard before the halfway point, but nonetheless, fans congratulated him as if he had won the race. The next week, he showed up again with his battered machine repaired enough to compete and won going away. He was victorious hundreds of times in modified stocks at such tracks as North Wilkesboro, North Carolina; Martinsville, Virginia; Raleigh, North Carolina; Columbia, South Carolina; and Spartanburg, South Carolina.

On September 11, 1949, Turner won his first official NASCAR race at Langhorne, Pennsylvania, driving a 1949 Oldsmobile. The next year, he won races at Martinsville, Charlotte, and Rochester, New York. He also won the pole position for the very first Southern 500 at Darlington (South Carolina) Raceway.

Turner was widely recognized for his business savvy, due in part to his silver sales tongue and overwhelming self-confidence. Many investors wanted to make deals with him, including Bill France. Turner teamed with France in the Mexican Road Race, an event that spread over 2,176 miles of rugged terrain. They were third after the fourth leg until a flat tire sidelined their efforts. Turner was disqualified for changing cars late in the race. But his stellar driving style was the talk of the race.

Turner won the 1956 Southern 500 going away. It was one of his biggest wins, and it served as a large stepping stone to his notoriety. He also won 22 of 43 Convertible races that year. It was truly a highlight season of his career.

In the 1958 Rebel 300 at Darlington, Turner and Joe Weatherly banged hard against one another down the length of the straightaways in factory-supplied Fords while company executives looked on in anger. The two called those types of side-bangs "pops"; thus, the nicknames "Pops" Turner and "Pops" Weatherly were born. After that race, the two called each other and everyone "Pops." The pair became inseparable friends.

Turner could be as taciturn as talented. Once while driving for team owner Glen Wood at Riverside, California, Wood asked Turner to

sit down in the seat to check the fit. Turner stuck his right foot through the window to the center of the seat and said, "It's just right."

On another occasion, Turner and Weatherly boarded a plane with their "party guests." They landed and rented cars to "race" down the highway. The cars were wrecked and smoking when returned to the car rental agency. Neither driver could rent a car in the state of South Carolina for many years thereafter.

Aside from a successful driving career, Turner engaged in the building of Charlotte Motor Speedway in North Carolina. The venture was a disaster, as much of his money was sunk into the 1.5-mile, high-banked racetrack. Unexpected rock beds slowed progress and caused thousands of unbudgeted dollars to be spent for large quantities of dynamite. Overtime pay and bad weather sent the speedway into near collapse before completion. Stockholders were screaming for dividends. The track broke up miserably during the inaugural running of the World 600 in 1960. Everything was going wrong. And Turner was deep in debt, with no money men to bail him out.

Turner approached Jimmy Hoffa of the Teamsters' Union for money in return for organizing the NASCAR drivers. France got wind of the plot and successfully put a stop to it, but banned Turner for life, along with fellow driver Tim Flock. By July 31,1965, Turner and Flock were reinstated by France to help build lagging ticket sales. Turner's return race came on October 31 of that year at North Carolina Motor Speedway in Rockingham, which translated into his 17th and final career victory. Flock, bitter with France over the banishment, never again drove in NASCAR.

Charlotte Motor Speedway eventually recovered from its woes under the direction of Richard Howard. Turner's partner in the venture, O. Bruton Smith, eventually resurfaced to return to power by the mid-1970s.

After his final win, Turner continued to look for the elusive ultimate money-making deal and was very quiet on the racing front. Aside from an occasional start in stock cars, he seriously took up golf in hopes of finding a career to follow when he was too old to hustle a race car.

It all came to an end on October 4, 1970. Turner, along with golf pro Clarence King, perished in a private airplane crash on the side of a mountain near Punxsutawney, Pennsylvania. Many theories concerning the cause of the crash continue 27 years later.

Curtis Turner contemplates a March 27, 1966, event at Atlanta Motor Speedway. His Wood Brothers Ford finished 13th after falling out with engine problems late in the race.

Left to right, Turner and Ralph Moody

Turner at speed in a Smokey Yunick Chevrolet at Atlanta on August 7, 1966.

left: Turner battles closely at Hickory, North Carolina, in the Holman-Moody Ford but in the end finished second to David Pearson.

below: Turner takes a nap before the start of the inaugural American 500 at North Carolina Motor Speedway held on October 31, 1965. Four hours later, he rested again in victory lane.

# RUSTY WALLACE 1956-

When a bushy-haired Rusty Wallace brought a Roger Penske-owned Chevrolet to Atlanta Motor Speedway on March 16, 1980, the Fenton, Missouri, native wasn't supposed to have much of a presence. After all, he was a rookie and it was his first Winston Cup event. But on that day, he mixed it up with the veterans of the sport and made it look easy.

Wallace was leading with 29 laps to go when 1979 Rookie of the Year Dale Earnhardt passed him for the win. Still, Wallace held on for second. That sensational debut was an early indication of a brilliant career.

Before he ever turned that first lap on the high banks of Atlanta, his credentials were already impressive. He won 1979 rookie honors in USAC competition and was 1983 ASA (American Speed Association) champion. Throughout the Midwest, Wallace established himself as a strong threat to win anywhere he raced. He entered select Cup races, hungry for a ride in the big show.

Winston Cup team owner Cliff Stewart tapped Wallace for NASCAR's elite circuit in 1984 and Wallace captured Rookie of the Year honors. His first victory came in his 76th career start on April 6, 1986, at Bristol Motor Speedway. In 1989, he was crowned NASCAR Winston Cup champion with team owner Raymond Beadle. Wallace fell short of winning his second Winston Cup title by only 24 points to Bill Elliott in 1988.

Wallace joined Penske again in 1991 as an established winner. His best years in the victory category were 1992 and 1993, when he logged 18 wins in 62 starts. All told, he's enjoyed 47 wins throughout his 17-year Winston Cup career.

At the end of the 1996 season, Wallace won the inaugural Suzuka Thunder 100, a special non-points event held in Suzuka, Japan.

Wallace is considered one the hottest stars in Winston Cup racing. Year after year, he is

A fast pit stop on September 3, 1989, lets Wallace stay in the lead lap. He finished fourth that day in the Southern 500 held in Darlington, South Carolina.

---

*Before he ever turned that first lap on the high banks of Atlanta, his credentials were already impressive.*

---

constantly demanding more and more perfection from his crew. With crew chief Robin Pemberton preparing his cars and calling the shots on pit road, the team is always a threat to score another championship.

Wallace and Penske, a longtime motorsports magnate who has enjoyed much success in Indy car racing, know the chemistry is always there for success.

"As far as learning about life and about business, my association with Roger Penske would definitely be the highest point in my career," Wallace once said of his longtime friend and team owner. "As far as accomplishments, winning the Winston Cup championship in 1989 was a huge accomplishment.

"I want to be remembered as one of the most serious and fierce competitors out there, who was always up front and who was a constant winner."

On February 14, 1993, at Daytona Beach, Florida, Rusty Wallace smiles for the CBS TV camera.

# DARRELL WALTRIP 1947-

**D**arrell Waltrip emerged on the NASCAR scene in 1972, the year President Richard Nixon was reelected. While turmoil brewed on the nation's political front, Waltrip was creating a little controversy of his own among the stock car racers of the deep South.

NASCAR Winston Cup racing had just celebrated its 24th birthday, a mere infant compared to professional stick-and-ball sports. Considered nothing more than an ambitious regional sport, NASCAR needed a vehicle to carry it into the big league sports arena.

Waltrip was just what the sport needed, a Kentucky gentleman whose words were as smooth as the liquor produced in the state's mountain region. Vibrant and flamboyant, he was never one to keep his thoughts to himself. His actions—a controversial rub here, a questionable driving style there—ensured that he stayed in the limelight.

Waltrip's plan from early on was clear: make his presence known among the established stars of the sport by sharing headlines with them or creating his own, at least until he could prove he was the better driver—to both fans and foes. He was known to find the empty microphone, tap its cover to get the crowd's attention, shout out predictions, then back them up with action. His tactics were usually as effective as scratching one's fingernails across a chalkboard. One could always count on Waltrip's name to be in the newspapers.

At times, fans expressed their dislike for him, but such behavior never unnerved him. He reasoned negative attention was better than none.

Waltrip's first victory came on May 10, 1975, using a car he built himself. From week-to-week, he was running consistently among the sport's big guns and building himself as an underdog who was holding his own against the big money drivers. He was given a chance at one of the prominent rides, that of the struggling but well-financed Digard Racing Company. Waltrip was heavily criticized for making the move, but in time, he backed up his words with actions and made the team a winner 26 times during a five-year span.

A contract dispute with Digard owners Bill and Jim Gardner in 1980 threatened to curtail or end Waltrip's career. He paid big money for the times, $325,000, to settle the dispute out of court.

The grass, and the money, were definitely greener with team owner Junior Johnson. Waltrip needed Johnson's winning ride to pay the large debt he had incurred.

Waltrip takes his Monte Carlo through the fourth turn at the Charlotte Motor Speedway during the UAW-GM Quality 500 held October 6, 1996.

> Vibrant and flamboyant, he was never one to keep his thoughts to himself. His actions—a controversial rub here, a questionable driving style there—ensured that he stayed in the limelight.

Waltrip had arrived once he slid through the window opening of Johnson's Buicks. Their teaming produced three Winston Cup championships, one in 1981, one in 1982, and one in 1985. Having gained center stage as champion made him as loud as ever.

In 1987, Waltrip left Johnson to drive for Rick Hendrick and scored six more victories, including his lone career Daytona 500 triumph in 1989, the win he calls his biggest.

Age and experience toned Waltrip down a bit by 1990, so much so he was voted Most Popular Driver in Winston Cup competition two years running. People were listening to him as the wise, elder statesman. Having been awarded NASCAR's Most Popular Driver gave him a distinction he had longed for his entire career.

In 1991, Waltrip formed his own team, and right out of the box, began to establish his organization as a winner. There were wins at Martinsville, Virginia, and the prestigious Southern 500 at Darlington, South Carolina, in 1992. All was going according to plan.

Then, as if a dark cloud stationed itself over him, his Chevrolets fell to the back in the past five seasons. Even though Waltrip has made personnel changes, car changes, and crew chief changes, the problem persists today. Through the help of former colleges like Jeff Hammond and Waddell Wilson, Waltrip continues to look to find success by going back to fundamentals.

Eighty-four victories are listed by his name in the record books, 16 shy of the goal of 100 wins he set for himself as a brash kid. More than likely, the goal will not be met. Still, there are plenty of accomplishments to cherish.

"People have asked me if I could pick out one particular event in my career that meant the most. I would say winning the 1989 Daytona 500 was very special, but as far as choosing the ultimate accomplishment, I can't really pinpoint one thing as the best," Waltrip says. "I like to look at the whole picture.

"I'm just thankful that I came into the sport at the right time. When it's all over, I want to look back and say that I made a difference by being in Winston Cup racing. I would hate to think I would look back at 25 years and discover no one cared."

Darrell Waltrip giving last minute instructions to his crew before race time in the fall of 1988.

On February 17, 1974, Waltrip takes his Chevrolet through the turns in the Daytona 500 and finished seventh in his second season of Winston Cup (then Grand National) racing.

left below: Waltrip after a hot day at Talladega on August 7, 1977.

At the Daytona 500 Waltrip does his famous "Icky Shuffle" to celebrate his February 19, 1989, victory.

Waltrip shows his disappointment after parking his Bud Moore Engineering Ford because of engine failure at Rockingham, North Carolina, on October 21, 1973.

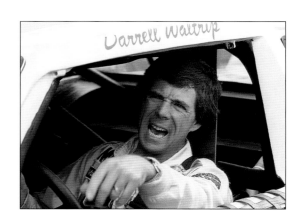

With things not going just right in the spring of 1982, Waltrip offers a few suggestions.

Waltrip is all smiles after winning at Rockingham, North Carolina, on October 20, 1985. Two races later, he was crowned Winston Cup champion for the third time in his career.

# JOE WEATHERLY 1922-1964

The only thing missing from Joe Weatherly was the clown suit and funny shoes. The rest was there, at any given moment in time.

Whether at straight up 12 noon or 4 A.M., he was the clown prince of stock car racing. He took nothing seriously, not even the strong suggestion to wear shoulder harnesses on that fatal January day in 1964.

His climb into stock car racing was his second on a motorsports tour, as he was already a three-time American Motorcyclist Association national champion between 1946 and 1950.

He raced not only to win, but also because he gained much-needed attention.

By 1951, he was wrestling with the bigger stock cars. Over the next two years, he logged 101 wins and his first modified championship. He joined NASCAR's Grand National (now Winston Cup) circuit in 1955. He ran mostly on the short-lived Convertible division from 1956 through 1959. In four seasons of Convertible racing, he never won the championship but finished second, third, fourth, and seventh, respectively.

Weatherly ran for the Grand National championship in 1962 and 1963 and won back-to-back titles.

Weatherly was the ultimate practical joker. Once he called the late Bob Colvin, former president of the Darlington (South Carolina) Raceway, in the middle of the night. When Colvin answered the phone, Weatherly asked, "Hey Pops, What are you doing?" Colvin calmly replied, "Oh, not much. I was just sitting here on the side of the bed, waiting on some son-of-a-bitch like you to call." Weatherly doubled over laughing and hung up. His mission was complete. The call came two days before his last laps in a race car.

On occasion, he would show up at Daytona with a pair of pants with legs of different colors. Weatherly even drove his race car during practice wearing a Peter Pan suit.

Weatherly and fellow driver Curtis Turner were inseparable. They raced hard against one another and partied even harder after the race was complete. Both were known for spiking the water jugs they carried in their

Weatherly (8) and Fred Lorenzen (28) fighting hard at Darlington Raceway on September 3, 1962.

> Off the track, Weatherly and Turner weren't beyond racing and destroying rental cars in the early morning hours. What was left of a few of them ended up in the deep end of more than one motel swimming pool.

cars. The pair often beat and banged on one another for hundreds of laps, then walked away laughing.

All told, Weatherly has 37 victories in NASCAR competition, counting the Convertible division.

Off the track, Weatherly and Turner weren't beyond racing and destroying rental cars in the early morning hours. What was left of them ended up in the deep end of more than one motel swimming pool.

On January 19, 1964, Weatherly was killed during the 87th lap of the Motor Trend 500 at Riverside, California. His Bud Moore-owned Mercury slammed driver's side first, hard against the steel retaining wall in the sixth turn, taking his life instantly. Had he chosen to wear the shoulder harness, many speculate he would have survived the crash. The sudden impact caused his head to strike the wall after the brakes failed.

"We had had some transmission problems with the car that day in Riverside," Moore says. "He had come into the garage, and we put a new transmission in. He was several laps down but went back out and ran the race. Later, I heard he had wrecked, but I couldn't see him from where we were in the pits. We were packing up tools, and I remember being called on the P.A. system to go to Les Ritcher's office. Les was in charge of the speedway then.

"When I walked into his office, he told me Joe had been killed in the wreck. I thought he was joking. I could hardly believe it. I just stood there and couldn't speak."

Joe Weatherly sports a look of determination before the start of an event in the early 1960s. He was killed in a single-car accident at Riverside, California, in 1964.

# GLEN 1925- LEONARD WOOD 1934-

The careers of Glen and Leonard Wood began under a large beech tree in the small community of Buffalo Ridge, Virginia. The tree's sturdiness came in handy when the need arose to pull out race engines in the early Modified and Sportsman cars. Glen eventually built a small garage at the home place to house his new career. The team has moved its location three times since, as the Wood family became one of the most successful organizations in all forms of motorsports.

Glen Wood was one of five original partners who pooled their resources and bought a race car. Before all was said and done, the only remaining partners were Glen Wood and Chris Williams, a local sawmill owner who loved racing. Of the two, Glen Wood became the driver, a thought that had never crossed his mind in the beginning. That is, until he saw a good friend racing at the Morris (Virginia) Speedway and felt he could do as well. Wood took his personal car out onto the speedway and was doing a fair job of keeping up with him. The person he was chasing was none other than Curtis Turner, who later became one of NASCAR's biggest stars.

Wood had only raced the car a few times before disaster struck. He and younger brother Leonard were towing the 1950 Ford back to Buffalo Ridge. The car had sustained heavy damage during the race, the worst being a bent rear end housing. On the way home, the rear axle broke, which contributed to the gas filler neck hitting the pavement. The car was quickly engulfed in flames and burned to the ground right in the middle of the highway. It was the first of many cars to be totaled over 40 years of racing.

In 1955, Glen Wood became the sole owner of the team by buying out Williams' portion of the team, but he called his team Wood Brothers Racing. Siblings Clay, Delano, Ray Lee, and Leonard were all once part of the team. Leonard has remained with the organization from day one. He is known as one of the most talented mechanics in NASCAR history.

The Wood Brothers found early recognition for their ability to make lightning-fast pit stops. Time after time, they proved they were the best at four tires and 22-gallons of fuel, often servicing a car in just over 20 seconds. Such quickness wasn't the standard in the early 1960s. Ford Motor Company executives asked them to crew for the late Jimmy Clark in the 1965 Indianapolis 500. Clark won the race going away, mostly

Glenn Wood at the Asheville-Weaverville Speedway on August 17, 1958. He started 4th and finished 24th.

The Wood Brothers' race team at Atlanta in the early 1970s. Glen Wood is on the extreme left, while Leonard is third from the right.

The list of those who took the wheel of Wood Brothers' cars reads like a Who's Who of motorsports: Curtis Turner, Junior Johnson, Fred Lorenzen, Marvin Panch, Dan Gurney, Tiny Lund, Cale Yarborough, Parnelli Jones, A. J. Foyt, Donnie Allison, David Pearson, Neil Bonnett, Buddy Baker, and Dale Jarrett are just a few who have helped to generate the team's 96 career victories in over 850 starts.

because of the Woods' skillful work in the pits.

Wood won dozens of short track races before retiring from driving in 1964. Much of the reason was his dislike for the superspeedways. Wood didn't mind leaving that chore to someone else. When it came to any track more than three-fourths of a mile in length, Glen was satisfied to stand on the sidelines. The list of those who took the wheel of Wood Brothers cars reads like a Who's Who of motorsports: Curtis Turner, Junior Johnson, Fred Lorenzen, Marvin Panch, Dan Gurney, Tiny Lund, Cale Yarborough, Parnelli Jones, A. J. Foyt, Donnie Allison, David Pearson, Neil Bonnett, Buddy Baker, and Dale Jarrett are just a few who have

helped to generate the team's 96 career victories in over 850 starts.

A few of their biggest victories have come in the Daytona 500. In 1963, while substituting for the injured Marvin Panch, Tiny Lund won the 500 after a spirited battle with Holman-Moody driver Fred Lorenzen. In 1968, Cale Yarborough won the 500 driving a Wood Brothers car and defeating Lee Roy Yarbrough, both men driving as if every lap was the last. Their side-by-side battle still ranks as one of the best in history. In 1976, David Pearson won the 500 in a Wood Brothers car after crashing with Richard Petty on the final lap. While Petty struggled to get his car fired after it stalled in the infield grass, Pearson had the presence of mind to keep the clutch engaged and rolled over the start-finish line at just over 20 miles per hour.

Today, Glen continues to head the organization. Leonard continues as crew chief, while Glen's sons, Eddie and Len, as well as daughter, Kim, are all owners of the team. All are an integral part of the team's success.

In earlier decades, the Wood Brothers were considered strong contenders for the win, week in and week out. Some of their best years came between 1972 and 1979, when driver Pearson logged 43 victories of 143 starts.

left: Dan Gurney gets some last minute advice from Leonard Wood prior to a race at Daytona.

Cale Yarborough (center) stands alongside the Wood Brothers' crew prior to the start of the Daytona 500. They gathered again later that day in victory lane.

On July 4, 1972, David Pearson makes a stop during the 1972 Firecracker 400 at Daytona. With six laps remaining, the Spartanburg, South Carolina, driver passed Richard Petty and Bobby Allison for the win.

# CALE YARBOROUGH 1939-

**W**illiam Caleb "Cale" Yarborough drove stock cars at 200 miles per hour simply for the thrill of it. Compared to his day-to-day antics, his racing career of 31 years seemed a bit tame.

Yarborough grew up near Darlington, South Carolina, in the small town of Sardis, a stone's throw from stock car racing's first superspeedway. At 1.366 miles in length, Yarborough covered every inch of it on foot at 10 years of age, searching desperately for some type of break in the wire fence that would allow him to sneak through.

Two years later, he competed in his first race, a soap box derby event, but complained afterward to his mother, Annie Ray Yarborough, that there was no motor and how they wouldn't go fast enough. Less than a week later, his father, Julian Yarborough, was killed in a small airplane crash. Young Yarborough found himself feeling much older than his age suggested.

A member of his local 4-H club, Yarborough roped a calf, raised it, and sold it, simply to raise money for an old car he wanted to buy. He built an old shed to house his investment and spent many hours rebuilding it. That led to constructing jalopies to race at such tracks as Sumter and Hartsville, thanks to financing he begged his mother to give him. Many nights, the single light cord burned in Yarborough's makeshift shed while he straightened what he wrecked the night before.

At 18, Yarborough couldn't discount his itch to drive at Darlington any longer. More times than the speedway announced a driver's name over the public address system, Yarborough had been shooed away from the garage area and the Pontiac to be driven by close friend Bobby Weatherly. On race day, when all officials were preoccupied with prerace duties, Yarborough slipped behind the wheel of Weatherly's Pontiac. He started 44th, finished 42nd after experiencing mechanical trouble, and earned $100.

Since that remarkable day at Darlington, Yarborough has found himself in much tougher circumstances than battling drivers twice his age around a one-groove racetrack, whether he was diving into swamps atop unsuspecting alligators, fishing water moccasins out of their homes with his bare hands, jumping from airplanes more than 200 times, or wrestling a pet

Yarborough pits during the 1968 Southern 500 at Darlington Raceway en route to victory. Note the crew members pulling sheet metal off the right front tire.

---

He once landed an airplane in a field without any prior experience and has been struck by lightning twice and lived to tell about it.

---

bear given to him by one of his pit crews, a bear that almost got the better of him. He once landed an airplane in a field without any prior experience and has been struck by lightning twice and lived to tell about it.

With short track racing offering him little and his chances for stock car racing's biggest arena nowhere in sight, Yarborough turned to turkey farming but failed miserably at his venture. He then moved to Charlotte, North Carolina, and found work at Holman-Moody, creators of Ford Motor Company's race cars. He swept floors, turned wrenches, anything he could do to keep the bills paid. Yarborough finally got a chance to drive one of the cars he helped pit crew and turned in an impressive showing.

Yarborough eventually drove for the best in the business; Banjo Matthews, the Wood Brothers, Junior Johnson, M. C. Anderson, and Harry Ranier gave him good enough equipment to log 83 victories in 559 starts. While driving for Johnson, Yarborough became the only driver in NASCAR history to win three consecutive Winston Cup championships in 1976, 1977, and 1978.

Yarborough retired from driving in 1988 and has fielded his own Winston Cup team for the past 10 seasons.

Yarborough's greatest personal accomplishments came with winning five Southern 500s at his home track, Darlington Raceway.

"There were a lot of great times in my career, but winning the Southern 500 five times is probably the most special part of it," Yarborough says. "I went over the fence once at Darlington (1965), but overall it's been a good track to me. It was, and still is, my home track, and I really enjoy going back there, even as a car owner."

Cale Yarborough won his first superspeedway at his home track in Darlington, South Carolina, on September 2, 1968. He was almost wiped out by heat and humidity.

Yarborough (11) leads Darrell Waltrip (88), James Hylton (48), and Bobby Allison (behind Waltrip) to the line at Rockingham, North Carolina, on February 29, 1976, before eventually finishing third.

left: Yarborough sports the cool head apparatus under his helmet after a long afternoon at Talladega, Alabama, on August 7, 1977.

Yarborough enjoys his moment in victory lane after winning his second Daytona 500 on February 20, 1977.

Yarborough enjoys an early victory.

left: Yarborough takes his Wood Brothers Ford to victory at Atlanta on March 21, 1968.

On September 6 at the 1965 Southern 500 held at Darlington Raceway, Yarborough went over the guard rail after coming together with Sam McQuagg. No one was hurt. Yarborough approached Banjo Matthews (car owner and builder) and said, "I broke your car."

While working traffic at Atlanta Motor Speedway, Yarborough wheels his Ranier Racing Chevrolet to victory on March 27, 1983. The car was originally built as a show car but was pressed into service when his primary car crashed.

Yarborough explains the highlights of his illustrious career.

# LEE ROY YARBROUGH 1938-1984

Even though great wealth and fortune placed Lee Roy Yarbrough in NASCAR's brightest lights for a time, unfortunate tragedy overshadowed all of his accomplishments.

Some blame stock car racing for handing him some such pain and grief. The true answer to that question died with Yarbrough on December 7, 1984.

His was a rocky road that produced a reputation for being a cocky, brash, and quick-to-anger loner who struggled to present himself in a manner acceptable to those within racing circles. The hot and cold attitudes he possessed haunted him throughout his career and overshadowed an exceptional talent.

Born September 17, 1938, Lonnie Lee Yarbrough was the oldest of six children reared by Lonnie and Minnie Yarbrough of Jacksonville, Florida. "Lee Roy" had a deep-felt fascination with auto racing by the time he turned 12. He often told school classmates he was going to build race cars for a living. Writing tablets filled with pencil-drawn racing machines instead of the required English and math assignments caused more than one note to be sent home to his parents.

At 16, he built his first race car, a 1933 Ford street roadster. By the 10th grade, the urge to race had overtaken him. He left Paxson High School his sophomore year, figuring he'd had enough formal training. Yarbrough hired a friend to drive the car in some races, but watching him handle the turns prompted the car's owner to climb aboard. Yarbrough won a main event at Jacksonville Speedway in his first turn behind the wheel.

Yarbrough aligned himself with Julian Klein, a longtime race sponsor and track owner in the Jacksonville area. The result was more than 100 wins in the local Sportsman and Modified ranks and Yarbrough's reputation as being unstoppable.

As time went on, Klein became more and more disillusioned with his driver, even though wins in his equipment were standard. Yarbrough was never on time, was hard headed and unmanageable, and carried an attitude. During an event at Savannah, Georgia, Yarbrough started shouting obscenities at the officials from victory lane and was disqualified for unsportsmanlike conduct. Klein fired Yarbrough after the incident.

Yarbrough resurfaced and won the Modified-Sportsman 250 at Daytona International Speedway in 1962 and followed up with 37 wins in the NASCAR Late Model Sportsman competition in 1962. He was eager to move into NASCAR's biggest arena, the Grand National

*Lee Roy Yarbrough finds a unique way to show off his young son, Lee, prior to race time during the summer of 1970.*

division. He entered 12 races that year and 14 the following year, with little success to speak of.

By 1964, Yarbrough was victorious twice with wins coming at Savannah and Greenville, South Carolina. His first superspeedway win didn't come until 1966, but prior to that victory, he became the first driver to break the 180-mile-per-hour mark, doing so in a Ray Fox-prepared Dodge. Yarbrough and Fox picked up $10,000 from NASCAR for being the first to break the speed barrier.

After teaming with car owner Jon Thorne in late 1966, Yarbrough's biggest win to date came on October 16 at Charlotte Motor Speedway. But troubles were brewing behind the scenes over money, and Thorne fired him by season's end. Before they parted company, Yarbrough and crew chief Mario Rossi engaged in a violent dispute. Yarbrough came after Rossi with a wrench, but the fight was broken up when Rossi pulled a gun and threatened to shoot.

Yarbrough then tried his hand in the Indianapolis 500 of 1967, first in cars owned by Gene White. After crashing hard in one of them, he quit White's team and joined Jim Robbins the next year. He started 26th and finished 27th with little fanfare.

He returned to NASCAR and team owner Bud Moore for six events beginning in June 1967, but he joined Junior Johnson by October of that year. It was a marriage that brought him his greatest success in auto racing.

The 1968 season saw a total communication gap between Yarbrough and crew chief Herb Nab. Races were lost because the crew chief and driver misread their own signals and either pitted too early or too late. There were two victories and six pole positions by season's end, but the struggle nearly broke them apart.

In 1969, Johnson changed Yarbrough's number from 26 to 98 in hopes of putting the less-than-desirable season behind them. The year started off rocky at Riverside, California, but it turned around quickly. Yarbrough won the Daytona 500, the Permatex 300 Sportsman race preceding the 500, the Rebel 400 at Darlington, South Carolina, the Firecracker 400 at Daytona, the Dixie 500 at Atlanta, and the Southern 500 at Darlington.

Then came the beginning of the end.

Yarbrough crashed hard at Texas World Speedway in 1970 during tire tests and was rendered unconscious. A few days later, fellow driver Cale Yarborough picked him up at his Columbia, South Carolina, home and flew him to Martinsville, Virginia, for the NASCAR race there. Weeks later, Yarbrough couldn't recall the flight home from Texas, the flight to Martinsville, or the race held at Martinsville. Many in the sport began noticing subtle signs of Yarbrough's strange behavior at the tracks.

Yarbrough shows the aftermath of winning the Rebel 400 at Darlington Raceway on May 10, 1969. In his left hand is the reason such a battle is worth the struggle.

Sporadic appearances in both stock cars and Indy cars followed. He was again involved in a hard crash, this time in an Indy car owned by Dan Gurney prior to the 1971 Indy 500. Shaken but not seriously hurt, he left the track and Indy car racing for good.

From June through November 1971, Yarbrough was in and out of hospitals after supposedly contracting Rocky Mountain Spotted Fever around Easter. During one 43-day hospital stay, he was reported near death with a fever of more than 105 degrees. Other reports cite the hospitalization for alcohol abuse. Neither diagnosis has been proven conclusively.

In 1972, good finishes in poor equipment came, prompting some to think he would return to his winning ways. Such a scenario didn't happen. His last start came on September 24, 1972, at Martinsville, but he wrecked after 109 laps. It was his last appearance in a race car of any kind.

On February 13, 1980, Yarbrough snapped. At 6:40 P.M. that evening, he violently attacked his mother, nearly choking her to death. Since 1977, there had been several incidents of lapses in memory and violent behavior, resulting in numerous arrests. Doctors said too many crashes in race cars inflicted the former driver with organic brain syndrome, a nonpsychotic secondary to craino-cerebral trauma. The condition had been heightened, they believed, by alcohol abuse.

On March 7, 1980, Yarbrough was judged incompetent to stand trial for attempted murder and was committed to a Florida mental hospital. On August 27, 1980, Yarbrough was found innocent by reason of insanity and continued to remain in mental hospitals, both in Florida and North Carolina.

On December 6, 1984, Yarbrough suffered a violent seizure while in a Florida mental hospital and fell, striking his head. He was rushed to Jacksonville's University Hospital where he died at 1:38 A.M. on December 7 from subdural hematoma, or internal bleeding of the brain.

**145**

# HENRY "SMOKEY" YUNICK 1923-

Henry "Smokey" Yunick grew up the hard way, without the benefit of a father and little information about his birth. It is believed he was born on May 23, 1923, around Maryville, Tennessee, but no documentation exists. He was supposedly given three first names; Henry, Harry, and Gregory, and eventually chose Henry.

He and his parents, John and Lena Yunick, moved near Philadelphia when he was still in diapers. A sister three years his junior was born there.

During the Great Depression, plowing by mules and horses was a way of life for those who farmed. For young Henry, those plowing chores began at morning light and ended long after dark.

The fact Yunick only completed the 10th grade is deceiving, considering he is known as one of racing's greatest mechanical geniuses. He left school to go to work and help support his mother and sister, making $5 per week in an automotive repair shop. He soon discovered he had an overwhelming talent for building and inventing.

Before he reached his 13th birthday, the horse he used to power his hand-driven plow died. Yunick assisted with the burial and immediately proceeded to remedy the problem for good. He built a motor-driven tractor from junk parts. A few days later, he was back plowing again. It was the beginning of decades of mechanical wizardry.

In 1939, Yunick tried his hand at motorcycle racing at a local half-mile dirt track. The motorcycle smoked heavily during the races, but it still managed to perform well week after week. Friends quickly dubbed him "Smokey." Thus, the nickname was born.

He served in the military during World War II and worked as a B-17 fighter pilot with the 97th Bomb Group. While flying over Daytona Beach during a training exercise, Yunick expressed his desire to live there, having noticed the beauty of the landscape from high above. After his discharge from the service, he first moved to Camden, New Jersey, but the bone-chilling winters quickly prompted him to move to Daytona by 1946. He hooked his small mobile home to the rear of his car and headed south.

Unable to find work, he began repairing the cars owned by people in a nearby mobile home park. He helped a blacksmith build springs in return for shop space and called his garage, "Smokey's—The Best Damn Garage In Town." Within months, he was servicing cars and trucks from all over the country.

*One of the craftiest tuners in NASCAR history, Smokey Yunick, built some of the most innovative—not to mention controversial cars that appeared on the NASCAR circuit.*

Yunick watches his car at the Daytona 500 with Andretti aboard on February 27, 1966.

After coming across a Cadillac owner who didn't want to pay for the extensive modification work he had performed, Yunick changed his sign to read, "Trucks Only!" The Cadillac was the last passenger car he ever serviced.

When NASCAR was born on the beaches of Daytona, it was a bit hard for Yunick to ignore the speed and excitement it generated. Soon, he was under the hoods of race cars, meeting the challenges stock car competition had to offer. Even in his earliest days in motorsports, his crude demeanor and salty language could be a bit intimidating. It proved to be the basis of his colorful character and legendary style.

Yunick made a habit of bending the rules as far as possible. Once he built a 1966 Chevrolet Chevelle that carried several tricks to its body and chassis, including a ridge at the rear of the top that created a spoiler and a front bumper that was extended several inches in depth. Yunick built the car over the winter months between the 1967 and 1968 seasons, and contracted pneumonia in the process.

Once he arrived at Daytona International Speedway for the 1968 Daytona 500, he was handed a list of 13 things that had to be changed on the car, the first being the floor pan. There was no way to fix the car in time for qualifying, which was to begin in less than an hour. Yunick finally jumped in the car and drove it back to his hauler. A story

written at the time falsely reported that the gas tank was removed from the car, creating another wonderful Smokey Yunick racing tale. It is only a myth, however, as the gas tank was still on the car.

From 1952 through 1975, Yunick fielded race cars for some of the best drivers in the business. On 10 occasions, he prepared cars in the Indianapolis 500. His stock cars entered 76 NASCAR races from 1955 through 1969. Winners in his cars were Herb Thomas in 1955 and 1956, Paul Goldsmith in 1956, 1957, and 1958, and Marvin Panch in 1961. His last victory as a team owner came during a 40-lap event at Daytona International Speedway on February 22, 1963, with Johnny Rutherford behind the wheel.

His best season came in 1954 as chief mechanic for Thomas, the owner and driver who captured the NASCAR car owner championship that year. Thomas later drove Buicks and Chevrolets owned by Yunick in 1956.

After retiring from racing, Yunick continued to sell and maintain trucks and invested in oil stock as well as work with alternative-fuel engines.

**147**

After driver Curtis Turner parked on a pit road with a distributor problem on August 5, 1966, Yunick jumps in head-first to check it out.

Yunick (left) discusses strategy with his driver Mario Andretti on February 27, 1966. In the end, Andretti started 39th and finished 37th.

In the summer of 1965, Yunick makes last-minute adjustments to one of his engines before placing it in the race car.

Yunick at Charlotte Motor Speedway for the inaugural
running of the World 600 on June 19, 1960.

# MORE GREAT MOMENTS

Buck Baker poses beside one of his early modified Fords during the summer of 1948, just after the start of his lengthy career.

Banjo Matthews (left) is shown with Fireball Roberts after the pair won a convertible race held August 17, 1958, at the Asheville-Weaverville Speedway. Roberts drove the 1957 Chevrolet 370 laps, with Matthews relieving him for the remaining 130 laps.

right: Joe Lee Johnson of Chattanooga, Tennessee, won the first World 600 held at Charlotte Motor Speedway. Johnson started in 20th position and scored his only significant victory on June 19, 1960. Johnson is joined in victory lane by an unidentified beauty queen and track owners O. Bruton Smith and Curtis Turner.
*Charlotte Motor Speedway*

Driver Marvin Panch cools off at the 1965 Atlanta 500.

Better known for his phenomenal success as a team owner paired with Dale Earnhardt, Richard Childress competed from the driver's seat since the mid-1960s. Childress started his first Winston Cup race in 1969, with 188 starts in his career. His best finish was a third-place outing in 1978.

left: A long-time driver for Richard Petty, Jim Paschal is shown here at the American 500 in Rockingham, North Carolina, on October 29, 1967. He started in 12th but crashed and wound up 35th.

left: In one of his select NASCAR appearances, Mario Andretti wins the 1967 Daytona 500 while driving for Holman-Moody.

Team owner Bondy Long cleans the windshield during the 1968 Southern 500 held at Darlington. Fred Lorenzen (right) is watching. Bobby Allison drove Long's 1968 Ford that day but dropped out with engine troubles after 41 laps.

On August 4, 1968, "Little" Bud Moore parks in the garage area to the taste of a soft drink and studies the laps he just turned at Atlanta Motor Speedway while with team owner Bondy Long.

Charlie Glotzbach's long NASCAR racing career began in the 1960s. Even as late as the early 1990s, Glotzbach could be found behind the wheel of a stock car from time to time.

Bud Moore contemplates information from a crew member while at his Spartanburg, South Carolina, shop in 1969. Moore was a car builder and owner, and his cars have carried a huge number of top drivers.

Pete Hamilton answers questions from victory lane after his win at Talladega, Alabama, on August 23, 1970.

Frank Warren in August 1977.

Country music singer and part-time race driver Marty Robbins enjoys a trip to Daytona International Speedway. Robbins died from a heart attack in 1982.

Just as is the case in Indy car competition, A. J. Foyt was victorious racing stock cars at Ontario, California, on March 5, 1972. Like Andretti, Foyt drove only a few select NASCAR races.

Michael Waltrip, younger brother of Darrell Waltrip, sits in the Bahari Racing Pontiac and listens intently to some advice before attempting to qualify at Charlotte Motor Speedway in 1988. Waltrip won "The Winston" of 1996, a special non-points event held at Charlotte Motor Speedway.

Terry's younger brother, Bobby Labonte, sits behind the wheel of his Joe Gibbs Racing Chevrolet in 1996. The Texas native has five career victories in Winston Cup competition.

Harry Gant's most prestigious win came at the 1985 Southern 500. Gant's string of runner-up finishes earned him the nickname "Bridesmaid Harry." When he started winning, he couldn't stop, reeling off a string of victories. He logged 18 victories before retiring in 1994.

The late Harold Kinder was a long-time NASCAR flag man who traveled the circuit for many years. Kinder was extremely popular with fans and participants alike. He had his own fan club and would sign nearly as many autographs as some of the drivers.

The late Elmo Langley found it was too expensive to field his own cars and signed on as crew chief for Cale Yarbrough Motorsports and later worked as a NASCAR official as the pace car driver. He suffered a heart attack and died in November 1996.

Ray Fox has prepared cars for some of the great names in racing, including David Pearson and Buddy Baker.

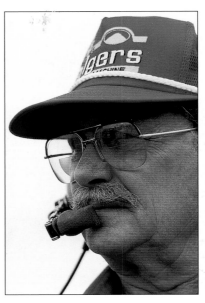

Harry Hyde was one of the great NASCAR crew chiefs, working with drivers such as Neil Bonnett, Buddy Baker, and Bobby Isaac.

Geoff Bodine captures a 125-mile qualifying win at Daytona for Junior Johnson. Four years earlier, he won the 500 while with team owner Rick Hendrick.

Car dealership mogul Rick Hendrick brought a make-it or break-it attitude to his entry into NASCAR racing and, as any race fan knows, he made it big. A list of Hendrick drivers reads like a who's who of racing, with Tim Richmond, Benny Parsons, Jeff Gordon, Terry Labonte, and Geoff Bodine being just a few of the elite group of drivers that have driven Hendrick cars.

Robert Yates has been with NASCAR since his days as an engine builder for Holman-Moody. He moved on to work for Junior Johnson, Parky Nall, and Digard before becoming a team owner with Davey Allison at the wheel. Known for his skill as an engine builder, Yates had Ernie Irvan and Dale Jarrett driving for him in 1997. Kenny Irwin will replace Irvan for the 1998 season.

Tim Brewer launched his NASCAR career with then driver Richard Childress. Here he is shown as a crew chief for team owner Junior Johnson in the late 1980s.

Jack Rousch was heavily involved with sports car racing before coming to NASCAR with driver Mark Martin in 1982. A hands-on owner, Rousch has successfully fielded multi-car teams, with drivers such as Wally Dallenbach and Jeff Burton.

# INDEX

Allen, Francis, 58
Allison, Bobby, 8, 10–13, 64, 68, 137, 141, 153
Allison, Bobby, 9, 17, 27, 39, 49, 65, 73, 89, 91, 109
Allison, Clifford, 10
Allison, Clifford, 9
Allison, Davey, 10, 13–15
Allison, Davey, 9, 15, 55, 61
Allison, Donnie, 16–21
Allison, Donnie, 9, 17, 49, 135
Allison, Eddie, 17
American Motors Matador, 12
American Motors Matador, 85
Anderson, M. C., 23, 93, 139
Andretti, John, 103
Andretti, Mario, 23, 49
Andretti, Mario, 51, 147, 148, 152, 157
Arrington, Buddy, 61
Bahari Racing, cars owned by, 158
Baker, Buck, 150
Baker, Buck, 23, 61, 63, 119
Baker, Buddy, 18, 22–25, 158
Baker, Buddy, 23, 81, 91, 115, 135
Ball, Ralph, 61
Ballard, Harold, 91
Balmer, Earl, 91
Beadle, Raymond, 109, 127
Benton, Bill, 49
Bernard, Mellie, cars owned by, 63
Bernstein, Kenny, 115
Bodine, Geoff, 159
Bodine, Geoff, 65, 89
Bonnett, Neil, 15, 27, 61, 65, 97, 135
Bonnett, Neil, 26, 27, 158
Brewer, Tim, 159
Brickhouse, Richard, 45
Brickhouse, Richard, 45
Brodrick, Bill, 68
Brooks, Dick, 17, 33
Bud Moore Engineering, cars owned by, 130
Buick Regal, 89
Cale Yarborough Motorsports, 158
Calhoun, Rory, 29
Castles, Soapy, 28–31
Castles, Soapy, 29
Champion, Bill, 115
Chester, Ted, 43
Chevrolet Chevelle, 87, 147
Chevrolet Monte Carlo, 129
Chevrolet Monte Carlo, 65, 87
Childres, Kennie, 109
Childress, Richard, 153, 159
Childress, Richard, 27, 33, 115, 117
Clark, Jimmy, 49, 135
Colvin, Bob, 133
Connerty, Hugh, cars owned by, 47
Cronkite, Will, 33
Cruise, Tom, 109
Cunningham, H. B., 87
Curb, Mike, 61, 103
Dallenbach, Wally, 103
DePaolo, Pete, 49
DePaolo, Pete, cars owned by, 111
DeWitt, L. G., 93
DeWitt, L. G., cars owned by, 95
Dierenger, Darel, 61
Digard Racing Company, 33, 115, 129
Dodge Daytona, 18, 28
Dodge Magnum, 101
Donlavey, Junie, 55, 93, 97, 115, 117
Duvall, Robert, 109
Earnhardt, Dale, 27, 33, 47, 55, 61, 73, 93, 97, 103, 109, 115, 127
Earnhardt, Dale, 32, 34–37, 89, 153
Earnhardt, Ralph, 33, 57, 91
Earnhardt, Ralph, 34, 90
Economaki, Chris, 67
Elder, Jake, 51
Ellington, Hoss, 17, 61

Ellington, Hoss, cars owned by, 15, 97
Ellington, Hoss, cars owned by, 21
Elliott, Bill, 38–41
Elliott, Bill, 39, 65, 71, 109, 127
Elliott, Buddy, 43
Eubanks, Joe, 91
Evans, David, 101
Farmer, Red, 15
Finch, James, cars owned by, 27
Flock, Tim, 42, 43, 51
Flock, Tim, 43, 123
Ford Coupe, 43
Ford Coupe, 57, 63
Ford Thunderbird, 27
Ford Torino, 39, 45
Fox, Ray, Sr., 158
Fox, Ray, Sr., 23
Fox, Ray, Sr., cars owned by, 23
Fox, Ray, Sr., cars owned by, 97, 145
Foyt, A. J., 157
Foyt, A. J., 17, 97, 135
France, Bill, Sr., 43, 45, 123
France, Bill, Sr., 44, 45
Freelander, Eric, 61
Gant, Harry, 158
Gant, Harry, 63, 73
Gardner, Bill, 9, 33, 129
Gardner, Jim, 9, 33, 129
Gazaway, Bill, 17
Gibbs, Joe, 61
Gibbs, Joe, cars owned by, 158
Glotzbach, Charlie, 154
Glotzbach, Charlie, 65, 91
Goldsmith, Paul, 23, 49, 147
Gordon, Jeff, 46, 47, 159
Gordon, Jeff, 47, 61
Gray, Henley, 33
Gregg, Peter, 91
Griffith, Andy, 29
GT40 Mark II, 49
Gunderman, Gerry, 89
Gurney, Dan, 135, 145
Gurney, Dan, 136
Hagan, Billy, 73, 87
Hagan, Billy, cars owned by, 74
Hamby, Roger, 87, 89
Hamilton, Bobby, 103
Hamilton, Pete, 156
Hammond, Jeff, 129
Harkey, Bob, 29
Harper, Robert, cars owned by, 17
Hefner, Frank, cars owned by, 57
Hendrick Motorsports, cars owned by, 117
Hendrick Motorsports, cars owned by, 73
Hendrick, Larry, 85
Hendrick, Motorsports, 109
Hendrick, Rick, 159
Hendrick, Rick, 47, 73, 93, 109, 115, 117, 129
Hodgdon, Warner, cars owned by, 27
Hoffa, Jimmy, 123
Holman Automotive, 49
Holman, John, 48, 52, 53, 78
Holman, John, 9, 49, 93, 97
Holman, Lee, 49
Holman-Moody, 152
Holman-Moody, 49, 77, 93, 97, 135, 139
Holman-Moody, cars owned by, 49
Holman-Moody, cars owned by, 77, 98, 99, 112, 113, 125
Howard, Mack, 57
Howard, Richard, 121
Howard, Richard, 9, 65, 123
Howard, Richard, cars owned by, 11
Hutcherson, Dick, 49
Hutcherson, Dick, 99
Hyde, Harry, 25, 59, 158
Hyde, Harry, 57, 109
Hylton, James, 141
Hylton, James, 17

Ingle, Bill, 115
Irvan, Ernie, 54, 55
Irvan, Ernie, 55, 61
Isaac, Bobby, 56, 58, 59, 158
Isaac, Bobby, 57, 91
Jackson, Leo, 93, 117
Jackson, Richard, 73
Jarrett, Dale, 40, 60, 61
Jarrett, Dale, 61, 135
Jarrett, Ned, 57, 61, 63, 77, 91, 111
Jarrett, Ned, 62, 63
Joe Gibbs Racing, cars owned by, 158
Johncock, Gordon, 23
Johnson, Joe Lee, 151
Johnson, Junior, 11, 27, 64, 66–69, 75, 110, 159
Johnson, Junior, 33, 57, 61, 63, 65, 73, 77, 87, 91, 93, 111, 115, 135, 139, 145
Johnson, Junior, cars owned by, 15, 27, 71, 129
Johnson, Junior, cars owned by, 58, 64, 75, 78
Jones, Parnelli, 23
Kiekhaefer, Carl, 9, 43
Kinder, Harold, 158
Klein, Julian, 145
Krauskopf, Nord, 23, 27, 57, 85
Kulwicki, Alan, 70
Kulwicki, Alan, 71
Labonte, Bobby, 158
Labonte, Bobby, 61
Labonte, Terry, 47, 61, 65, 73, 109
Labonte, Terry, 72, 74, 75, 159
Langley, Elmo, 158
Langley, Elmo, 29, 117
Larson, Mel, 73
Lentz, John, 63
Long, Bondy, 57
Long, Bondy, cars owned by, 10, 153, 154
Lorenzen, Fred, 49, 61, 65, 77, 81, 135
Lorenzen, Fred, 53, 76–79, 133, 153
Lovern, Mike, 109
Lund, Tiny, 80, 82, 83
Lund, Tiny, 81, 135
Manning, Skip, 73
Marcis, Dave, 17, 33, 85
Marcis, Dave, 84, 85, 107
Marlin, Clifton "Coo Coo," 87
Marlin, Sterling, 65, 87
Marlin, Sterling, 86, 87
Martin, Mark, 88, 89
Martin, Mark, 89
Mast, Rick, 159
Matthews, Banjo, 57, 139
Matthews, Banjo, 58, 150
Matthews, Banjo, cars owned by, 17
Matthews, Banjo, cars owned by, 17, 18, 142
Mattioli, Joe, 109
May, Dick, 73
McCall, Fred, 53
McClure, Larry, 55
McDuffie, Paul, 111
McQuagg, Sam, 142
McQuagg, Sam, 91
McReynolds, Larry, 15
Means, Jimmy, 61
Melling, Harry, 39
Millikan, Joe, 73
Mock, Butch, 27, 85
Moody, Ralph, 48, 50–53, 124
Moody, Ralph, 9, 49, 77
Moore, Bud, 154, 155
Moore, Bud, 9, 23, 39, 57, 91, 93, 97, 115, 145
Moore, Bud, cars owned by, 33, 133
Moore, Bud, cars owned by, 35, 130
Morgan-McClure Racing, 87
Morgan-McClure Racing, cars owned by, 55
Nab, Herb, 145
Nab, Herb, 68
NASCAR, founding of, 45

Negre, Ed, 33
Negre, Norman, 71
Nichels, Ray, 97
Nichels, Ray, cars owned by, 57, 85
Nichels-Goldsmith, cars owned by, 84
Osterlund, Rod, 33, 97
Owens, Cotton, 66, 90, 91
Owens, Cotton, 91, 97
Owens, Cotton, cars owned by, 23, 24, 96
Pagan, Eddie, 51
Panch, Marvin, 153
Panch, Marvin, 49, 77, 81, 91, 135, 147
Parrott, Todd, 61
Parsons, Benny, 39, 49, 93, 97
Parsons, Benny, 93–95, 159
Paschal, Jim, 153
Paschal, Jim, 23, 49, 91
Passino, Jacques, 49, 93
pe2, 101
Pearson, David, 23, 27, 29, 49, 57, 73, 91, 93, 97, 103, 135
Pearson, David, 96, 98, 99, 125, 137, 158
Pemberton, Robin, 127
Penske, Roger, 9, 39
Penske, Roger, cars owned by, 85, 127
Petree, Andy, 117
Petty Enterprises, 23, 103
Petty Enterprises, cars owned by, 23, 24
Petty, Kyle, 100, 101
Petty, Kyle, 55, 101, 103
Petty, Lee, 29, 63, 91, 101, 103
Petty, Maurice, 101, 103
Petty, Richard, 17, 29, 47, 63, 71, 73, 85, 101, 103, 135
Petty, Richard, 21, 101, 102, 104–107, 137, 153
Presley, Elvis, 29
Pryor, Richard, 119
Purcell, Pat, 57
Rahilly, Bob, 27, 85
Rahmoc Enterprises, 109
Ranier Racing, cars owned by, 143
Ranier, Harry, 9, 15, 23, 93, 139
Ray, Johnny, cars owned by, 33
Reagan, Ronald, 65
Reno, Mark, cars owned by, 55
Rexford, Bill, 47
Richmond, Tim, 109
Richmond, Tim, 35, 108, 159
Ritcher, Les, 133
Rivers, Mendell, 45
Robbins, Jim, 145
Robbins, Marty, 156
Robert Yates Racing, 55
Roberts, Fireball, 110, 112, 113, 150
Roberts, Fireball, 49, 77, 91, 93, 111
Rogers, Bob, 109
Rossi, Mario, 9, 145
Rossi, Mario, cars owned by, 11
Roush, Jack, 159
Roush, Jack, 89
Rudd, Al, Sr., 115
Rudd, Ricky, 55, 114, 115
Rudd, Ricky, 73, 115
Rutherford, Johnny, 47, 109, 147
Sabates, Felix, 101
Sauter, Jim, 89
Schrader, Bill, 117
Schrader, Ken, 116, 117
Schrader, Ken, 117
Scott, Wendell, 118–121
Scott, Wendell, 29, 119
Shuman, Buddy, 112
Shuman, Buddy, 29, 49
Smith, Jack, 97
Smith, O. Bruton, 123
Smith, O. Bruton, 151
Stacy, J. D., 33, 89, 109
Stacy, Jim, 27
Staley, Gwyn, 63

Stark, Ralph, 9
Stavola Brothers Racing, 87
Stavola, Bill, 9
Stavola, Mickey, 9
Stephens, Jim, cars owned by, 111
Stewart, Cliff, 127
Stewart, Jackie, 47
Stott, Ramo, 45
Strickland, Frank, 111
Stricklin, Hut, 65
Stroppe, Bill, 43
Sullivan, Jack, 53
Talladega Torino, 98
Terry, Bill, 71
Thomas, Herb, 49, 147
Thompson, Jimmy, 57
Thompson, Speedy, 29, 63
Thorne, Jon, 145
Tinsley, John, 91
Trickle, Dick, 63, 89
Turner, Curtis, 122, 124, 125, 148, 151
Turner, Curtis, 43, 49, 77, 123, 133, 135
Turner, Tommy, 49
Ulrich, D. K., 55, 89, 109
Unser, Al, 91
Unser, Bobby, 49
Vallo, Chris, cars owned by, 97
Vandiver, Jim, 45
Vaughn, Linda, 67
Wade, Billy, 91, 93
Wallace, Rusty, 126, 127
Wallace, Rusty, 47, 127
Waltrip Darrell, 17, 65, 71, 73, 115, 129
Waltrip, Darrell, 41, 128–131, 141
Waltrip, Michael, 158
Ward, Bill, 69
Warren, Frank, 156
Weatherly, Bobby, 139
Weatherly, Joe, 49, 93, 123, 133
Weatherly, Joe, 78, 132, 133
Wheeler, Humpy, 83
White, Gene, cars owned by, 145
White, Rex, 103
Whitmore, James, 29
Williams, Chris, 135
Wilson, Rick, 103
Wilson, Waddell, 129
Wilson, Waddell, 50
Wlodyka, Roland, 33
Wood Brothers, 23, 27, 49, 97, 101, 139
Wood Brothers, 60, 100, 135, 137
Wood Brothers, cars owned by, 27, 122, 142
Wood Brothers, cars owned by, 61, 81, 93, 97, 135
Wood, Glen, 134, 135
Wood, Glen, 17, 27, 97, 123, 135
Wood, Leonard, 135, 136
Wood, Leonard, 17, 135
Yarborough, Cale, 15, 49, 61, 65, 73, 81, 93, 115, 135, 139
Yarborough, Cale, 68, 98, 137–143, 158
Yarborough, Cale, cars owned by, 61
Yarbrough, Lee Roy, 11, 20, 144, 145
Yarbrough, Lee Roy, 17, 29, 135, 145
Yates, Doug, 103
Yates, Robert, 15, 55
Yates, Robert, cars owned by, 15
Yates, Robert, cars owned by, 61
Young, Buddy, 93
Yunick, Smokey, 146–149
Yunick, Smokey, 49, 57, 111, 147
Yunick, Smokey, cars owned by, 125
Yunick, Smokey, cars owned by, 147
Zervackis, Emmanuel, 61

*Italicized entries refer to photographs and captions. The page numbers listed contain the photographs; the captions may be on the adjoining page.*